History, despite its wrenching pain, cannot be unlived,
but if faced with courage, need not be lived again.

Maya Angelou

NAKED

Stripped by a Man and Hurricane Katrina

Julie Freed

A Memoir

JULIE FREED

Text © Julie Freed, 2014
First Edition
Also available as an ebook by Ant Press, 2014

For Jim and Laura who saved my life.
And for my daughter who kept me living.

CONTENTS

PART 1: ONE WEEK IN AUGUST

1 Things We Carry 3
2 Peeling Layers 10
3 Bright Spot 14
4 Red Flags 26
5 Landfall 29
6 It's a Wonderful Life 34
7 Roseman Bridge 52
8 My House 62

PART 2: STORM TRACKING

9 This Type of Certainty 65
10 Our Homes 73
11 Instinct 84
12 New York City 88
13 Genoa 93
14 Unforgettable 97
15 Happy Birthday, Baby! 108
16 Bridal Lane 112

PART 3: CLEAN UP

17 Fairytale 125
18 A Father's Wisdom 137
19 Rummaging 151
20 A New Normal 161
21 Dissolved 169
22 A New Year 172
23 The Anniversary 174
24 Keys 179

Epilogue 184
Contacts and Links 187

PART 1

One Week in August

They carried all they could bear, and then some, including a silent awe for the terrible power of the things they carried.

TIM O'BRIEN

The Things They Carried

1

Things We Carry

I carried Genoa onto the bedroom deck. She sat on my lap, my arms around her. I rocked in my chair, gently stroking her back. Happy, she played with the tag on a little plush cow in her lap. I looked at my swing hanging from the live oak, to the marsh grass, and across the bayou with its now empty boat docks. Everything moved to the wind's rhythm.

The hanging swing danced on my neighbors' pier. I saw Jim earlier when he removed the swing cushions, cleaned up his boat dock and crab traps. His wife Laura stopped over. We talked and decided to evacuate together to one of their local business properties. They had lived on the coast for decades and knew of storms all too well. They worked diligently all weekend too, bringing in any potential projectile. As I was alone with the baby, they helped me move larger planters and furniture into my garage.

Better neighbors one could not have. They treated me, a Yankee from New England, like family from the day I moved south. They hosted crab boils on Sunday afternoon. Mushrooms, celery, garlic, corn, potatoes, blue crabs boiled in a pot of bay leaves and Zatarain's. Garlic bread and beer washed it down. The aroma would waft to my house around noon, luring me. I could never leave grading papers until Sunday evening. I was too sleepy after the fresh air, warm company, and delicious Gulf food. "Just give them all A's!" Jim would joke.

3

Our neighbors were as unique as the homes on Bridal Lane. A retired sea captain lived two doors down. He grew up on one of the barrier islands and rowed a boat to school as a kid. He and his wife babysat Genoa when I taught a class in the evenings. They had three grown sons and loved pampering my little girl. Directly across the street lived Lily Grace, a noted Mississippi artist. I enjoyed a 5pm cocktail with her every now and then, while she walked me through a work in progress in her home studio. She shared stories of growing up in the Delta, her live-in help, her late husband, time on the coast, and Hurricane Camille. The unofficial "Mayor of Bridal Lane," a neighbor in the opposite direction would visit everyone on morning walks with his beagle. A brilliant couple across the street also from up north had three sons. They tried again for a daughter and had twin boys.

It was my coastal home. But now my house was in the path of a humongous hurricane while my husband made demands of me and my body.

Wednesday 24 August 2005

Earlier that week I received an email from Conner who was living in Miami Beach, Florida. He was stationed there with the military doing trauma training. It was early evening. After reading bedtime books to Genoa, I sat back down at my desk to re-read his disturbing email.

> *Julie,*
>
> *I know deep down you do not think I am a good person anymore. And I am sorry you are not happy. I am tired of all the arguing. My job is incredibly demanding and I do not think you get that … We both could probably be happier apart … I do not have a great family like you to depend on, but being alone seems better than hearing complaints all the time. I am not who I want to be anymore. I drink to numb the pain you cause me. You are pushing me to alcoholic tendencies and I need a change no matter the cost.*
>
> *Conner*

I sat blue-faced, alone. Motionless, I reread a pivotal conversation that I just realized was midstream. I reread the final sentences a thousand times. "Pain you cause me ... no matter the cost." I'd heard of people breaking up over email, but divorce after a seven-year marriage, a nine-year relationship, a home, a one-year-old child?

He didn't answer his phone that night.

Thursday 25 August 2005

Finally, in the wee hours, he called. He was calm, absent.

"I got your messages. I'm just returning your calls," he said. I searched for words in my half sleep.

"Um, I got your email." I paused. "I don't understand. Are you saying what I think you're saying?"

"Julie, well, I am thinking we would be happier with other people."

"Other people?" My faced squinted with bewilderment.

"You don't understand my work."

"So that means we should find 'other people?' Conner what is wrong? What is going on with you?"

"I'm just thinking we would be happier with other people."

"You mean *you* would be happier with other people?" I didn't allow him to respond. "Conner I don't have 'other people' on my list. We are married, to each other. I don't understand what you're going through right now. I'm sure Miami and the all the trauma you're seeing is extremely stressful. This email is just out of the blue, and I'm totally worried about you."

"I've had time to think here, Julie. I've been running every morning, clearing my thoughts. And I've been able to talk with new friends here."

"And you've decided you need me to be more sensitive to your work? I can do that, Conner. I'm sorry you feel neglected. It's tough being apart. I'm a single working mom with an infant and you're in Florida."

"Julie you know I will always care about you ... "

"Wait, you're not ending this conversation. We need to discuss the issues and all this 'pain' I'm causing you. I don't want to cause you or anyone pain."

"I just think that maybe we would be happier apart. And when I talk to other people about our situation they kinda think so too."

"What other people? Who are you talking to about *our* marriage?" My head shook, my eyes raced. "And why aren't you talking to *me*?"

"Sometimes it's easier to talk to friends. The friends I've made here understand me. They get my job."

"Well, Lucas works in the hospital with you. Yes, he understands your work more than I do. But these people don't know you, they don't know who you are, Conner. I know the real you. Genoa and I were there just a week ago, and everything was fine. We had a good time. We had good sex. You seemed happy to see me, tired, but happy. I'm completely shocked you're saying all of this. What's changed suddenly in a week? Is there someone else?"

"No, there's no-one else," he quickly replied. "Julie, look it's late. Let's talk about this in the morning, okay?"

"Can we go see a counselor when you get back home next month? Sort things out with help?"

"I think we're past that, Julie. We went to a counselor before."

"That was about your family issues more than about us. Let's go for us, for Genoa. You can help me understand. I want to help you, Conner. Your work is draining. You're barely sleeping. It's hard to think straight when you're so sleep deprived."

"Okay, we'll see. Maybe. Let's talk tomorrow."

"Okay, I love you, Conner. I have lots of packing to do tomorrow but call when you have time off. I wish life wasn't so hard for you right now. It will be better when you're home with us."

"Yeah … Okay … Bye." The phone clicked. He'd never said goodbye without saying he loved me.

I felt emptier and more confused after the one-sided conversation than before we spoke. I'd learned nothing. I pulled my laptop into bed and read his email again. I was exhausted but could not rest.

Friday 26 August 2005

Conner called midday after his hospital rounds. I'd been packing for evacuation and trying not to get anxious about his call.

"So I've been thinking about your questions. Asking what you could do to help me."

"Good that makes me feel better. So, what are your thoughts?"

"Well, you know I kind of have a thing for boobs. And I'm thinking it would really help me if you would have a boob job. You know not a real huge Dolly Parton one or nothing. But a few sizes bigger, you know." I imagined him holding his hand as if grabbing a breast while he spoke. I didn't know what to say.

"Okay," I hesitated. "Other thoughts or changes?"

"Well, Julie, I need more sex. You know I need it to stay calm and focused. So if we are going to stay married," I shuddered at his flippant comment, "I need you to *promise* you'll have sex every day."

He was all forthcoming with information today, as if he and his friends made a list during rounds. I'd never heard him make comments like this and was afraid to ask if there were more. Where was all this coming from? Who was brainwashing him?

"We aren't even living together right now. And with military assignments, it doesn't seem realistic. You know I won't make a promise I can't keep."

He became aggressive. "Why aren't you living here?"

"You know that's not fair Conner! The military condo with tile floors and balcony doesn't make taking care of a toddling baby easy. And the hot Miami sun on her tender little skin. Besides, I have a *job* here! I can't just pick up and leave for three months. You're not thinking straight. We discussed *all* this and planned *all* our visits before you left. None of the other wives moved there during the rotation. Where is all this coming from?"

"I just know now those are the things I need," he said flatly without responding to anything I'd just said.

"So you are saying that if I have breast surgery and promise to have sex with you every day, then we'll stay married?" I could not bring myself to say the D word.

"I don't know for sure. But it would be a start."

I blinked slowly. I was talking to a stranger with ultimatums. I felt like a counselor trying to pry information.

"Are there other things going on with you? Other things I should know?"

"I just think you'd be happier with someone else, Julie," he said, almost tenderly. "Maybe you should have a look around on Yahoo Personnels." He was so casual, like this was *normal* conversation for married people. I barely recouped before he asked, "Oh yeah, before I forget, can you get my wedding ring? It's on my dresser."

I hadn't realized he'd left it behind two months ago. Hit from all sides my head twitched at the bizarre comments. Our last conversation provided no information and now a surge.

"Okay, I've gotta get back to the patients." That was always his way of pseudo politely ending a conversation. "I'm glad we talked. Thanks for hearing me out. And thanks for gettin' that ring. That platinum's worth a lot, and I don't want it lost in the storm."

"Sure. All right. Have a good afternoon," I said mechanically. "I'll be home tonight if you want to talk. Bye."

Numb, deflated, of course I would be home tonight. My body heavy, I walked up the new staircase to our bedroom. At first, I didn't see his ring. Scanning the dresser-top back and forth, my eyes stopped at the figurine my sister gave us when Genoa was born. Titled *New Life*, the statue depicted a man holding an infant, admiring it with outstretched arms. Behind him, the wife and new mother hugged him around the chest looking over his shoulder in amazement at their new miracle. His ring was there. It was hooked on the infant's head as one would hang a hat on a rack. I saw the platinum circle and fell before his dresser. My fingers grasped the dresser's glass top, my body crumpled on the carpet, limp arms above me. A fierce shudder rolled down from my shoulders as a primal moan escaped from deep inside. My mouth hung open, staccato breaths. The deluge began. Fat tears burst from my eyes. My nose ran, face painted thick and wet. My hands anchored the dresser. I swayed as my shirt hung with sadness.

I stopped crying and stared at my hands now resting upon my moist pant legs. My wedding band circled my finger. I lifted my head, looked out the window above and heaved a heavy sigh. The cry did me good.

A wedding ring is forever, it should be worn forever and for always. I'm leaving the ring here. If it's not here when I get back, it's a sign.

"I will not be the one to carry your ring. That's your responsibility," I whispered.

His ring belonged where he had left it. I had carried much, but I would not carry that ring for him.

Time stood, calm rose. Perhaps I'd reached the eye of the storm.

2
PEELING LAYERS

Saturday 27 August 2005

My parents, traveling in Puerto Rico, had just returned to their Connecticut home. I'd not had an opportunity nor had I wanted to tell them about the divorce email yet. I wasn't sure Conner was in his right mind when he'd written it. Maybe this had been a knee-jerk reaction. But as our conversations continued, his words and plans became more defined. I began realizing he would soon end our marriage.

Compounding the situation, my parents were about to close on a house for their possible retirement in Mississippi. They were buying a house here to be close to us and their granddaughter. Now I would be divorced, and not own a house here but my parents would. They had returned from the bank when I got them both on the phone.

"Genoa and I are fine, but I have some bad news. Conner wants a divorce." I heard the subtle sucking in of air on the line. "He emailed last week. We've talked and talked, and emailed for hours over the past few days. Things might change, but it sounds like he's ready to walk. I don't know why exactly. But he did request I have a *breast enlargement* and wants me to *promise* to have sex with him every day." I flinched in embarrassment.

Not only because it was a horrible thing to share, *"Your son-in-law doesn't think my body is good enough,"* but because my mother was a breast cancer survivor. She'd had only one breast for over a decade. I cringed, saddened, imagining their faces, their expressions as they looked at each other. But I needed to get it all out.

"Things seemed fine during the visit to Miami and in the few days we had there after you all left. I mean he was his typical stressed self about the birthday party. But we certainly didn't talk about *divorce*! Things have been hard with him being away so much this past year. But I'm probably as surprised as you."

"Oh, Julie, do you think he'll go for some counseling when he gets back?" Mom asked.

"No," I answered. "It sounds like he doesn't even want to come back to the house, Mom. He's doing this all over email and phone, like he's ready to end things now, while he's away. I don't know what I can do. He doesn't sound like himself, that's for sure. I don't know if it's that friend Lucas influencing him, and the night life he's enjoying. It's such a crazy, sex-filled city. You were there. It's plastic world, hardly wife and baby reality stuff."

"Well, maybe I can talk to him," Mom said. "We've always had a good relationship. Would it be okay if I call him?"

"Of course, Mom, if you want to. This is all so hard. Maybe he'll at least give you some clue."

Nothing about my life or marriage could be private anymore. I would need help. Unveiling and exposing the truth was my only way to peace.

I consciously shifted the conversation to hurricane preparations and evacuation details. The concern and worry in their voices were palpable, but at the same time, their words and tone gave me strength, as they had always done.

"Julie, we'll get through this. We'll do whatever we need to do. We love you. One thing at a time right now," my dad said.

I exhaled as I nodded over the phone. "Thank you. I'm so sorry I had to tell you. It's all been *so* hard, especially with you buying the house here. Great timing, right? I feel bad about *everything*."

"Oh, please Julie. Don't worry about our feelings right now," Mom said. "Focus on what you need to do and get to safety."

"Julie, just take care of yourself right now," added Dad.

"Okay, well, let me go," I finished. "Still have lots to do here. I'll call soon with an update. I'm hardly sleeping. Please call anytime. Love you both so much."

We said our goodbyes. I wept. I wanted them with me. I wanted to take away their pain. I hated knowing they were hurting because of my pain and my husband's actions. Sad, scared, alone, I wanted to know what they were thinking. I wanted to talk with them more, but knew there was nothing else to be said. Yet I desperately wanted to be on the phone with them. I wanted to fast forward to next week and have this all behind me.

δδδδδ

Next, I called Conner's best friend from medical school. Gavin was now a radiologist in Washington D.C. Maybe he could talk to Conner, man to man.

Gavin called back in 30 minutes.

"Julie, it didn't even sound like Conner. But he seems pretty sure this is what he wants. He said he's thought it through. But he sounded too flat. I didn't even feel like I was talking to Conner."

"It's almost robotic, right? I've been hearing the same thing."

"Julie, I'm so sorry you're going through all of this. I don't know what is going on with him. Just wish I could do more to help. You know how much we love you guys. I can't *believe* he's doing this."

Our conversation continued as we searched for some logical explanation - alcoholism, drug use, bipolar disorder. What was happening to his friend, my husband?

Next I called one of my dearest friends and confidants, Nora. We met in graduate school in New York City. She grew up in Long Island and had the fabulous accent to match. We were both athletic females, pursuing mathematics, from good, hardworking Catholic families, with liberal social consciences. She married a wonderful Italian economist and had a daughter a few months older than mine. We shared everything about everything – well, almost everything. Some things had been too painful to share. I was ashamed and embarrassed by what had become of my marriage, my husband.

We didn't talk about it then, but I knew she remembered the time at their New York City apartment years ago, right after Conner and I got married in 1998. We'd gone to a bar after Nora and her husband made us dinner. Conner ended up drunk and vomiting on the floor of the *women's* bathroom. Our evening cut short, as we had to take him home.

Nora listened to me describe the emails, the phone calls – both the exhausting ones and the unanswered at Conner's Miami condo. I could see her face through the phone, brown eyes wide, hand to forehead, curly black hair pulled back. We cried together.

"Oh Jules, I wish there was something I could do. I mean you two were the best at our wedding. Conner is such a good guy. I'll never forget him with my parents, tying all those cans to our car. It was all so sweet. You guys are so sweet together. Jules, my God, all the romance. Maybe he's going through some weird thing, some phase or whatever. Who knows, maybe there's something going on with his family? You know how they can be. Maybe he'll get home and clear his head." Nora babbled on about our relationship and all the times the four of us had shared. She sounded shocked and surprised. I didn't know what to say, except that I loved her and knew she loved me.

Nora was one of the most brilliant individuals I had ever known, with incredible affection and gentleness about her. She was a Wall Street genius, a mathematician, a logician, and an efficient problem solver. Even though she knew about some of Conner's problems and his family issues, she was dumbfounded. And it was rare for her to be dumbfounded by anything.

Tired, tired of talking, and tired of trying to piece the puzzle together. These conversations were hard. I sought answers, but no solution existed. I heard the radio announcer.

Katrina is a Category 3 storm, predicted to become Category 4.
It is 380 miles from the mouth of the Mississippi.

3
Bright Spot

By late Saturday morning, August 27th most outdoor preparations were complete. I was tired.

Weeks ago, before Katrina threatened or Conner emailed for a divorce, an evening had been planned with a few friends from the university. We bought tickets for the Chris Botti concert. All were to gather at my house for wine and appetizers, then head out for sushi and the show. And now I wasn't sure I wanted to play hostess. Not sure I even wanted to go to the show.

I called Tara. She was coming down later for the show. She'd been divorced for years, a difficult divorce and ongoing issues with two teenage children.

"Conner wants a divorce."

"Why, what happened? Is he still in Miami?"

"Yes."

"Is there someone else?"

"I don't know. I don't think so. We've been living apart so much with the military. With his work away and my nights up and down with Genoa, it's not like we've had much of a relationship. But we all had a good visit when we were there about a week ago for Genoa's birthday. I don't really know what's going on. But something clicked for him suddenly."

"Julie, I'm *so* sorry. Want me to come over early this afternoon?"

"Please do. I really don't know what to do at this point. And I don't know that there's anything I *can* do. And with storm prep alone, I've got enough on my plate."

"I can probably be there around three. Want me to bring anything?'

"No, not at all. Just bring yourself and some hugs."

"Okay, Julie, hug that baby. Hang in there. I'll see you soon."

I looked forward to talking with Tara one-on-one and hoped to get some calm and wisdom from her divorce experience. It felt good to know I would have some companionship in the house besides the dog and Genoa. No one I knew well was divorced, except Tara – certainly nobody my age. Several of my close friends had never been married. I had not talked to anyone face-to-face about this yet. I was too embarrassed. I was ashamed. Ashamed my marriage was in trouble and embarrassed because I thought it was going pretty okay.

I was already different from the Julie of a week ago. I was exposed. The public failure of divorce felt so dirty to me.

I began imagining my life with only Genoa and steeling myself with thoughts and images of divorce. What would this mean for her in the future? I was so close to my father. He coached my teams, helped with homework, played catch, taught me to shoot pool, came to every concert, every play. Genoa wouldn't have that. She wouldn't have an encouraging male role model in her life, telling her, "You can do it!" She would only have me, a 'Single mother.' I said those words aloud. I was frightened.

A large part of me held onto the 'maybe he will change his mind and come to his senses' dream. If we had time alone, time to really talk about our lives in person, things might be different. I had these 'win him back' Hollywood images. But I realized, I didn't know who or what had taken him. Win against whom? Then I thought about his drinking, that afternoon on the shower floor.

δδδδδ

Tara's car pulled into the front half circle drive. Relieved to have another adult to talk to, I met her on the front porch. We hugged. It felt reassuring but also awkward, almost schmaltzy, and possibly premature. I floated along in a shifting surreal life. Waves of embarrassment washed over me. Why had I even shared the news? What if this was temporary? Conner had made rash decisions and sudden changes in the past, and then reverted.

Tara and I sat in the sunroom, eating grapes, cheese, and crackers, enjoying the broad view of the water. Our conversation danced over a variety of topics; work, divorce, her kids, her father's research as a meteorologist, and her grave concern about the hurricane. She told me her father thought the storm would destroy the entire coast. I listened, but I must have looked vacant because that's how I felt. Details of a variety of Florida hurricanes she had witnessed growing up and her predictions for the coast passed through me. I remembered Conner sitting in that same chair, lying straight into my eyes.

δδδδδ

Early evening my other friends arrived. I lit some candles, and we sat around two large, black, Chesterfield couches that faced each other. They were classic in style, and I loved them because they oozed academic charm and intellectualism. I loved reading on those couches, I loved breast feeding on them. They were always cool and clean to the touch, and my gold and red throw pillows drew the colors of a Casablanca print. Arranged in parallel to encourage conversation and debate, I loved them more than ever that night because of the setting they created. My witty, smart friends laughed, drank, and chatted about their lives and dreams of academic successes. Genoa ran about the cocktail ottoman in between the two couches grabbing snacks to munch and playing peek-a-boo around the couch ends. This was what I imagined when I created this little nook.

I sat on the arm of one of the couches by the bar so I could serve drinks. I realized how, instead of missing Conner, wishing he was there to share the evening, I was relieved he wasn't there. I didn't need him to finish my wine or end another fun evening on an embarrassing note as had happened too many times.

Calm entered and tension drained from my shoulders. Maybe it was the wine, maybe the companionship, maybe it was merely that I was able to savor the moment and relax for the first time in days and enjoy the present.

Maria, who'd grown up in Florida, asked, "How was your trip to Miami? And how's Conner?"

The mention of his name startled me a bit. I looked to Tara, sighed.

"Well, the trip was good. My whole family flew down for Genoa's birthday. But as of last Wednesday, he wants a divorce."

Eyes in the group opened wide. Some muffled gasps.

"I don't really know what's going on but he sounds pretty certain about all of this. So I guess we'll see," I said, raising my eyebrows and shrugging my shoulders. Everyone fell silent as I dropped the bomb followed, by a ripple of "I'm sorry."

"I'm looking forward to a fun evening and I'm sorry to dump that on you all. But it's much easier than keeping it in, frankly. I'll probably have to sell this great house. So let's enjoy it while we're here," I said, "and he's not."

Slight snarkiness was in my tone in the hopes of bringing levity. This was not his crowd, not his type of evening. I wouldn't have to work to compensate for him, his off comments, or badly timed jokes. I wouldn't have to worry about how much he was drinking and if he'd make it through the show. My evening would not be cut short because of him. I would have a fun night, divorce or no divorce.

The conversation was onto jokes about American men and their cultural obsession with breasts and then fun political banter about Southern women and their deceptively strong and creative tactics in dealing with men. I looked at the individuals smiling and laughing. I knew each person sitting around me had their own struggles in love; they shared those struggles with me, and they were laughing and smiling. Maybe it was okay to smile and laugh when it was dark and maybe it would even feel good. I'd not really slept for a week, but the moment was a fantastic bright spot after days of darkness.

I sat perched on the arm of my couch - a little mockingbird, head high, wine glass in hand. The candle light and the surface of my wine danced for a bit as Ella Fitzgerald sang in the background. I savored the moment, listening to my happy friends enjoy each other's company. I'd let go of a little of my shock and pain by sharing. I felt closer to these friends than ever before.

Unlike conversations earlier in the day, this group was ready to joke, prepare, and support me in battle, carry me into the next phase of my life. Maybe they knew me better than the others, perhaps knew my marriage better. Maybe they were more comfortable with the reality, since they had more experiences with love's failure. Or maybe because we were all together in person they could better sense what I needed and what they could provide as a group. I needed jokes about boob jobs and Miami Beach and egocentric doctors. I needed strong women to say to me, "This is crazy." "Conner's out of his fucking mind." "What an utter loser, dump that!"

Sushi, more good wine, and some soul filling music - Chris Botti's mix of blues, jazz, and classical energized my weary mind. I knew Conner wouldn't have enjoyed an evening like this. But for me, this was a perfect Saturday night.

During the show Botti talked about the 'Bitch who broke my heart, she even took my dog' sporadically during the show. The comments got laughs, of course. I joined along even though I was sharing his heartbreak. A truly touching performance that for me was a two-hour glimpse of hope and humor between the "divorce email" and the mandatory Katrina evacuation. I felt an affinity and affection for him that would last for years. We shared a deep personal moment, and yet he would never know. I suppose that's the beauty and wonder of being a performance musician. You impact people who listen to your music the world over and never know the extent of your touch.

Botti asked, "Do you know what the absolute sexiest city is?" I smirked and shrugged to my friend and colleague Benjamin when Botti said, "That's right, South Beach, Miami, Florida!"

Three days ago, Conner sent that email from Miami Beach. New York never sleeps but South Beach Miami never stops clubbing, partying, and cruising the strip. Genoa and I had visited every three weeks during Conner's trauma training at Miami Regional hospital. A plastic surgery center sat on every corner. If your nipples were covered, it was considered dressed. It was a difficult place to entertain a one-year-old. The summer sun was brutal, and the condo was shabby at best. Genoa and I enjoyed the pool and beach late in the day when the sun wasn't scorching her infant skin or we drove up the coast during the days when Conner was working or sleeping. The military put him up on the beach there, and he took advantage of the location. Our bank account was proof. His housing was paid for, food was provided at the hospital 24-7, but Conner managed to withdraw $400 a week for expenses and charge additional meals and gas. I couldn't imagine burgers that expensive, even in the sexiest city in the world!

Sunday 28 August 2005

After the show, I fell fast asleep, but only briefly. After days of house preparations, packing, rushing, talking, I wished I could sleep while Genoa slept, but I couldn't. I listened to National Public Radio as I lay in bed.

1 a.m. - Katrina is upgraded to a Category 4 storm with wind speeds reaching 145 mph. - National Hurricane Center.

Finally after hours of restlessness, I pulled the laptop off the nightstand and wrote Conner an email.

Conner,

I can't sleep, it's 3am. The storm is getting worse. I talked to Jim and Laura and we'll be evacuating with them. They have lived on the coast their whole lives and I know they'll know what to do. I think the storm is a Category 4 now.

But in the meantime I keep thinking about you, us, and everything from the last couple of days. My mind is just spinning. I listened to some voicemails you left just last week about how much you're looking forward to taking Genoa to Disney on our drive home from Miami. And then another about our trip to see fall colors in West Virginia in October. Less than a month ago when I was in Miami we were having sex, and good sex at that, celebrating our wedding anniversary.

I'm shocked, I'm sad, and this has all happened over the phone and by email which makes it all the more horrible and surreal. You know my family is a thousand miles away and I'm here alone taking care of our 1 year old. You wrote that you care for me and always will, but your words and actions are not that of a husband of 7 years or even a friend. I'm scared for you and hope you're okay.

As I said yesterday, I am SO worried about you and your future. Whatever you finally decide, Genoa and I will recover some day. We have a support system and a loving family. But where will you be - alone in a bar? And your comment about Yahoo personals was so odd. Why would I want or need to have a look around? You are my husband, Genoa's father I want to be with you. The thought of dating or being with someone else makes me nauseous – I want to be with you.

I sat in the light of the computer screen and reread my email. Foggy, I lay back down in bed with Genoa. I reviewed all the things I needed to pack for her and the dog.

The morning was spent packing short term items. Scrambled eggs, fresh and canned fruit, formula, water, snacks, wipes, diapers, toys, books, clothes for my baby girl. Food, bed, and treats for my dog Sweetie, overnight clothes and toiletries for me. I also left candles, water, flashlights, batteries, and a radio on the kitchen table for our return. We probably wouldn't have power for quite some time. Sometimes the back glass sliding doors leaked a bit when there was a hard rain especially at an angle driven by wind. I took the rest of the paper towel rolls in the house and piled them up by the doors to soak up leaks. Laura called to tell me she would cook a crock-pot of shrimp spaghetti for dinner. I would bring some red wine. We would need it.

We kept joking, "It's not SO bad. It's just mandatory camping."

But the storm was looking bad. Katrina was growing more and more immense, and evacuations were now required from Louisiana to Florida, almost 500 miles of coastline. I'd only lived on the coast for the last four years, but even the local newscasters and radio announcers were sounding anxious.

> *7 a.m. - Katrina is upgraded to a "potentially catastrophic" Category 5 storm. NOAA predicts "coastal storm surge flooding of 15 to 20 feet above normal tide levels."*
> *- National Hurricane Center.*

Conner and I moved to the coast so he could begin his medical residency. We both graduated in spring of 2001, he from medical school and I with my doctorate. I had a tenure track position at the university in the mathematics department. We purchased a beautiful waterfront home on the north side of a peninsula that was bordered on the south by the Mississippi Sound connected to the Gulf of Mexico and to the north, a large bayou. The homes were unique, and the centuries old live oaks garnished with Spanish moss, kissed by peninsula sea breezes, made the place a natural sanctuary. The name always drew cute comments when I gave my address over the phone - 'Bridal Lane.'

Now 'Bridal' as residents called it had water on both sides of the peninsula that was steadily rising all day. The skies were still clear, but the pelicans, egrets, and herons were not soaring as usual. They knew to evacuate as well. Mississippi public radio provided an update.

> *10 a.m. – With wind speed reaching 175 mph,*
> *NOAA raises their estimate of storm surge flooding*
> *to 18 to 22 feet above normal tide levels.*

Sunday afternoon I spent several tiring hours on the phone with Conner talking about our marriage. He talked again about my getting a breast enlargement and wanted me to *promise* to have sex with him every day. My post nursing breasts weren't good enough? Maybe I shouldn't have breastfed. Am I not sexy enough? Or maybe I didn't want to have sex with him enough. Maybe I wasn't attracted enough to him to satisfy his daily sexual needs. But we had a one year old, and we'd barely lived together over the past year due to the military assignments. Every day seemed excessive. Maybe this would all change when she was older, when I was at least sleeping through the night.

On a bungee cord I floated - then swinging, jerking, and falling. I was jerked hard and then left to float in a smooth, fuzzy haze. I reeled myself in, pride intact, head held straight again. I am Genoa's mother. Genoa - What does this mean for her and her future? The voices in my head chattered, continuously replaying our phone conversations, my last visit to Miami just ten days prior. Sometimes I thought, *He's joking, a man this smart can't really think our marriage will be fine with more sex and bigger boobs ...* It was hard to think about anyway. I was trying to evacuate from an enormous hurricane, take care of a one-year-old, and secure our home.

"Yeah, sure! Schedule me for a double D next Wednesday!" I found myself cocking my head in puzzlement that he could be so naïve and that I could have married someone so selfish.

I was Genoa's mother. She was part of me. I was David and Diane's daughter. I was a professor, a scientist, a doctor. What else? Was I Conner's wife? What did that mean? What did it mean to him? My whirling thoughts toyed with the idea of plastic surgery. But this was a short path. Where would it end? This year, improve this, next year, tuck that and plump this. I knew he was teasing me down a path I didn't want to go down. But I felt weak and wanted to save my marriage. My mind bombarded with information and storm preparations. I didn't have enough brain to remember and process it all. But I knew I did not want to be divorced. I did not want that shame on me or my Catholic family. Divorce was not in my vocabulary, not over things so trivial and temporal. *Domani! Domani!*

δδδδδ

I returned to the business of preparations. Packed the car to the brim with baby food, water, supplies, treasured items, all of our identification, insurance and mortgage papers, toys and books for Genoa, Conner's medical and military paperwork, laptops, cameras. I moved other equipment to high places in the home, brought all outdoor furniture, swings, and plants into the garage. I ran into town to withdraw more cash at the ATM. Town was eerie with only a few cars on the road, most stores and gas stations closed.

My wine was packed for dinner. I'd just bought a few hundred dollars of wine and liquor for our bar last week. I decided to bring the 'cheap' wine instead of the good Pinot Noir. Had I only known! Lesson learned: always drink the 'Good Pinot.'

I stood outside the garage. Paix Bayou had been rising all day but a sweet and salty calm was in the air. The rich earthy winds were delicious. I tasted the salt as I prepared the house. In previous days, police cruised up and down the street with megaphones telling people, "You need to evacuate by 4pm." Our street had immense live oaks that bowed and reached across the road. If they fell and blocked the street, emergency passage would be impossible. But that afternoon there were no cruisers, no megaphones. It was suspiciously desolate. Listen harder, and there was the whisper of imminent danger. Our street was silent, and I was numb.

The frenetic pace typical of my storm preparation absent, everything was packed. Genoa slept and the phone sat silent. I floated around the interior of my home, making sure I had everything *important*. A hazy task to determine what should be left behind.

Once complete, back up in our bedroom my feet warmed as I stepped into a sunlit portion of the plush carpet next to the French doors in our bedroom. We had created a peaceful space surrounded by sea and light. Our brand new master suite perched above the garage had water views from every one of its ten windows. French doors led to a deck with spiral stairs up to a crow's nest with 360 degree views of the coast and perpetual sea breezes.

I looked into the mirror above the dresser. My hair was shorter now. I smoothed my palms and fingers on my cheeks and face. My face was thin, cheekbones defined. No sign of baby weight. I'd lost that long ago with a hungry baby at my breast. I scanned my body's reflection, my neck, my collarbone, slender, pronounced. My arms tanned and toned, finished with tiny wrists, strong hands, and long slender fingers. These were my mother's hands. Veins and tendons becoming more pronounced and interesting each year, like hers.

The early evening light always made me slow down a bit. I paused to enjoy the pinks and golds flooding the earth. I made a note of time passing. I followed the sunlight reflecting off the inlaid glass of the dresser. A framed picture of Genoa in my arms, a small bowl created by a local potter friend, and the faceless wooden sculpture of the new family all sat together. I swallowed hard eyeing his ring again.

δδδδδ

The phone rang. Laura said they were ready to drive to our refuge for the night. We would only be a few miles from home, in one of their office buildings, able to return once the storm passed without traffic and delay. I did one last walk-through. I knew I'd already done all that I could with a car packed to the gills, garage crammed with outdoor furniture, plants, swings; paper towels and rags at the doors and windows, batteries, water, canned food, flashlights, candles for our return. Genoa and I would be safe. Nothing else mattered. It was time to go.

I drove away from 22 Bridal Lane. *Don't look back, Julie,* I told myself. I did not want to make the moment more dramatic than it was. I never looked back at the house I called 'home' for four years. I was ready to leave.

4
RED FLAGS

How was it possible that my neighbors cared more for our safety and well-being than my husband, the father of my child? In our conversation Gavin said, "I would be *swimming* from Miami to Mississippi to help my family at a time like this. I don't understand him." Conner knew I was extremely independent and self-sufficient. Perhaps he assumed I could handle this.

> Julie,
>
> Your mother called tonight. We had a good conversation. She told me you were safe so far. I am so worried about you and Genoa's safety. If the house is washed away, I don't even know what insurance companies we have, or where any of our investments are, or even where your life insurance is. That's how worried I am about you. It could all be gone and I might not have any records. Please write back if you get this.
>
> Conner

I didn't receive this email until days after the storm. But I spoke with my mother late that evening, achingly, intensely about her conversation with Conner. Laura and Jim were in bed, and we were all holed up in their office space awaiting Katrina.

"Julie, I don't know what to think. I just know I heard so many red flags in our conversation. His voice sounds calm, like he's made up his mind, but not completely, he said." She swallowed and sounded scared, almost crying. "He was telling me about all the 'positive outcomes' he had witnessed with breast enlargements." I swallowed heavily picturing Mom's prosthetic breast sitting on her dresser with a TV in the background delivering Hurricane Katrina warnings.

"Oh, Mom I'm so sorry. It's all so … "

"Yes, it is," she interrupted. "I didn't know what to say. But I did ask him if he would be willing to meet with me in October when he gets back home."

"And?"

"He would not agree to meet. He said he didn't want to return to 22. So I told him I'd meet him wherever. And that's when he said, 'my mind is made up, but my heart is not just yet.'" It was just like Conner to be so poetic, and I was somewhat boosted by his comment.

"Goodness, well, we'll have to wait and see I guess, Mom. Thanks so much for calling and asking him to meet. I really can't believe he would talk with you about breast surgery. He's so incredibly weird right now."

"I couldn't believe it either," she said flatly. I heard severe concern and distaste in her voice. She spoke unusually slowly and deliberately. The man on the phone tonight was her son-in-law, but she didn't recognize him either.

I changed the subject, hoping to bring her back to the immediate. "For now, Mom, we are safe. Genoa is sleeping. Jim and Laura just went to bed before I called. And tonight we talked for hours about everything. We drank some wine, ate spaghetti, and had some good laughs with Genoa. It's so sweet because she thinks this little house is so fun. She loves the sleeping-bag and all the office boxes to climb on. It's like an adventure for her. She's such a little light in all of this mess." Mom laughed a bit now. Genoa made us all smile.

"Yes, she is!" And I heard the smile in Mom's voice. "I'm looking at her picture right now on my fridge from your visit in February – that sweet little snow sled!"

"Alright, Mom, it's so late. I'm going to get some rest. And you too, okay? I'm sure you're exhausted from all of this and getting back from your trip, which I haven't even heard about yet!"

"You know, I don't require much sleep. The trip was wonderful. We are fine."

"I'll call tomorrow when I know more. This thing is supposed to be the worst early morning which is better than now or in the middle of the night. So we'll see. I'm going to cuddle with Genoa. Love you so much, Mom."

"Okay, love you, honey."

"Goodnight, Mom, love you, bye."

5

LANDFALL

Monday 29 August 2005

> *6 a.m. - Katrina made landfall on the Mississippi*
> *coast as a strong Category 4 storm, with sustained*
> *winds of nearly 145 mph and predicted coastal*
> *storm surge of up to 28 feet.*

My first panic attack struck. Heart pushed from my ribs and the arteries throbbed in my throat. My pounding chest was visible through my T-shirt. Katrina's winds raged outside the little brick building. It was 9am, and I needed to go lay down to try to catch my breath. Laura said she would watch Genoa. I lay on my sleeping-bag on the floor. The ceiling fan slow and hypnotic rotated above me. Rhythmic loud ticking of the pull cord whirred. My right arm cradled my head, the other hand on my stomach. The coffee still on my tongue, but my mouth was dry, my hands clammy. My heart raced faster. Radio voices faded in and out.

> *Do not leave your home. If you have not evacuated yet,*
> *do not leave your home. Widespread flooding across*
> *the entire area, anything south of I-10 is dangerous ...*

We were south of I-10. The night before, we looked out the back door to see I-10. All traffic was east bound. Now the interstate was empty. The skies were bright but heavy gusts of wind lifted the gutters of our little refuge. More radio voices.

> *Reports of tornadoes and touch downs in ... (static)
> ... we are currently on a generator, and we're going
> to stay with you as long as we can, giving whatever
> help and information ... shelters are open at the
> following locations, but again if you are safe and*
> *not in immediate danger, stay put until this thing is
> finished ...*

Spinning, I replayed my last conversation with Conner.

"Julie, I think you're all going to die. The Army Corp has predicted the whole coast will be flooded. Everything south of 10 will be gone. You're all going to die! I'm so worried about you. I don't even know where your life insurance policy is. And I don't know anything about our home insurance." Deep breaths.

I wondered what he was doing in Miami Beach. I wondered how my family was coping. Were they all watching the same news? A radio voice came across again. Barely audible, he broadcasted from a multi-level parking garage on the beach. The winds blew, and waves crashed loud. Between the background noise and static, Jim switched the radio off. I heard him say bleakly, "Enough for now."

I tried to relax. One year old Genoa asked Laura to color with her while she played in a cardboard box. Giggles, and the dog romping around the two of them. I felt guilty as I tried to rest.

My heart beat on the outside of my ribcage. Jim entered the one bathroom across from where I lay. This was doing me no good. Replaying, rethinking, rehashing, regurgitating. Done, I needed distraction.

The power went out.

I sat up, took some deep breaths, and evaluated. I had the Baby Bjorn with me. I could strap Genoa to my chest and swim out if needed. Sweetie would fend for herself and I could tie her leash to me while she swam beside us. We were across the street from a fire house that had a generator going with their lights on. Plenty of brawny men and women were there to help us if needed. I took a deep breath, my breathing still short. My Genoa would be okay.

My whirling mind only made my heart race faster. I stood. I'd rather be sharing small talk and nervous jokes with Jim and Laura. It was light outside so we could see the trees being pinned down by wind and small flying debris.

The winds howled. The gutters lifted. All the windows were boarded up but we opened the back door and saw I-10 in the distance, with not a car in sight. We were on high ground a mile or so from the Gulf of Mexico. Many times the storm seemed to subside completely, but then picked up again. Katrina rained and raged around our little house from early morning until almost 4pm.

Jim and I itched with impatience to get back to our houses and assess the damage. Since the storm had been ebbing and flowing all day, it was hard to tell if it had fully passed or not. We waited 20 minutes and decided Katrina was finished. We were ready to head back home. We snickered about whether we should bring our house keys or not. Perhaps the doors were blown open anyway? We shrugged and brought them.

Laura, Jim, Genoa, and I piled in their car and started driving south. Business signs were beaten by the wind, overhangs at gas stations mangled or forcefully removed. Debris covered the street, but it didn't seem too bad. Genoa fell asleep minutes after we pulled away.

We drove about half a mile and came over a small hill to meet Paix Bayou, a waterway parallel to the Gulf. Peninsulas in both directions covered with homes facing both north and south on both sides of the large bayou, stretching almost half mile wide. Large beautiful Mediterranean mansions, Southern antebellum homes - all under water. The waves crashed up the sides of the bridge we were about to cross. This was no longer Paix Bayou. It was the Gulf of Mexico. The Bayou had been engulfed. The raging waves of water seemed to be receding, but it was hard to tell anything when former landmarks were not visible.

We looked at ravaged houses. Entire homes were torn from their foundations. Walls ripped away exposing two floors. The private spaces – bedrooms, bathrooms – were on display without permission. That someone might have drowned, might be up the street – Genoa might have one day gone to school with their child. That someone could be me. The pain I felt was deep anguish and sadness.

Clothing strewn about and appliances floated in the water. Laura saw a bar stool she thought was theirs, but we were still over a mile from our homes. The private lives, the secrets of others, floated in the water before me. The chairs used for family dinners where everyone knew their place, the front porch swing where Papa sat, the chair Mama used to sit in and read to the children, the stepping stool used by generations at the kitchen sink, the fishing rods that Grandpa used. Naked. Suddenly we were naked. Everyone was naked. Lives exposed. I could see it all. I felt I should not be looking.

Parts of homes, parts of lives, floating, exposed for all to see. My family had always been so private and protective of our world. Katrina was hyper exposure, a complete revealing.

We three sat up as close to the car windows as we could. Jim leaned over the steering wheel as if in a race, yet he drove with extreme caution. He gripped the wheel, his hands' veins visible. He moved with caution and precision. Waves splashed onto the bridge as we crossed. The wind hammered us; full gusts felt inside the SUV. Giant veils of wind-driven water developed in the distance. Trees and marsh grass moved in its wake before reaching us. Amidst the chaos and reorganization of our world, there was a rhythm. Katrina's deep pulse beat heavily. We opened the car windows slightly and inched forward.

The air tasted delicious. I swallowed and felt her deep inside me, filling me up. She was full of energy. We were explorers in her world. She led us. The ominous excitement frightening and invigorating, teased us forward. We moved with care; we were respectful and vigilant. We knew we were not in charge. Jim was a protector, a business leader, a strong man, kind, and reverent, but like all of us, he was a follower now. He made sure we wanted to go forward, especially with Genoa in the car. But Laura and I agreed. We could not turn back.

6
IT'S A WONDERFUL LIFE

In the late 90s I was a graduate student. I sat at my cubicle desk doing long, hand-written calculations on the extended nonlinear Schrodinger equation. Little newspaper clippings were pinned over my cubicle wall, singles ads and crossword puzzles. I heard muffled snickering from the two guys on the other side of my cubicle wall. I pretended not to notice, sipped my coffee, and kept working. A few minutes later they walked by my glassed cubicle, presumably en route to the water cooler. Again I pretended not to notice.

I spent the summer of 1996 doing applied mathematics research for the US Government in Texas. My first year of graduate level studies in mathematics was behind me, and I had a competitive opportunity working for a government research group. Two guys, Rob and Conner, were entering their senior year in college. They were two years younger than I. Rob was dark haired, muscular, and Conner was almost blond, tall, slender. They had come to my office to ask if I was going to be on the office softball team. Multiple daily conversations ensued.

It was obvious neither had much experience around women, and their random, flirtatious communications were sweet in a goofy way. Over the next couple of weeks, I began making purposeful trips back to the biology laboratory area for softball team information or to pass along the menu for lunch orders.

No one else my age worked in the building, and we three became friendly. I learned they were both biology majors, hopeful med school students, both from small towns.

At our first softball game, I had the chance to talk in a more relaxed, non-work environment. They were nice enough guys, impressed with my softball skills. It's always fun to play on a pick-up office team, see all the outfielders move in when a woman is up to bat. My first up at bat I hit a triple over the centerfielder's head. Our season continued like this for a couple of weeks. They asked me to hang out after a few games, but I declined. Both started chatting with me a bit more when they passed my office.

They invited me again to have a beer after a game. The three of us chatted for an hour. Conner asked if I'd ever been in a Corvette.

I looked at Rob and back at Conner, eyebrows raised, and said, "No, I'm not exactly a car person. I'm a city girl these days. We take trains."

"So you've never been in a Corvette then?"

"No," I said, under-impressed. "I haven't. Not really my thing."

"Well, let's go for a ride anyway. It's a nice night."

I shrugged, looking at Rob and said, "Wanna go?"

He said, "Sure, go for a ride." We all walked out of the room, and Rob added, "I'll stay behind, you guys enjoy."

I was disappointed since I was more attracted to Rob.

"We'll see you when we get back then?" I asked. "We'll only be 15 minutes."

He nodded and waved.

Conner and I were alone for the first time. It was a cool Texas summer evening. Riding low in a sports car was kind of fun. He put the radio on, Celine Dion was singing one of my dad's favorites. The digital lights on the dash were modern looking. I asked a little about the car, making conversation.

"It's an '85," he told me. "I bought it used."

We got on the highway. He picked up speed and took an exit equally fast. Being so low in the bucket seats, the way the car held the road, it didn't feel dangerous at all. We were back within 15 minutes.

"Oh, where's Rob?" I asked.

"He's probably in his room now," Conner said. "Let me show you some pictures of my family."

"Okay." I thought this gesture sweet.

Conner showed me a picture of a handsome young couple who were his parents.

"They were both voted best looking in high school," he said. "That's when they met."

They looked more like his older siblings or cousins than his parents. He had two brothers, one older, the other an identical twin. His older brother was, " ... kind of quiet, and a mechanic, like my dad." I saw a soft, gentle side of Conner. He told me about the rigors of the military and his plans to go to medical school. I just listened to this sweet guy, asking probing questions as he talked periodically flashing me his big blue eyes.

"I had appendicitis when I was eight. My family doctor was so kind. He really got me through it all. I was so young, but he put his hands on me and I was at ease. I'd really like to be a small town family doc like that someday, help people one by one, just like he did for me."

Conner grew up in a little town in Oklahoma. His family was poor, but they were loving, hardworking people, he said.

"My parents had some troubles when the state built a new highway, and they were forced to move out of their home, but that was a while ago. They have a farm now. I go there for holidays and stuff."

I learned later he grew up on free school lunches. He was one of the kids in school with clothes that were worn and didn't exactly match. I saw pictures of him and his brothers when they were kids, three cute little blond boys, who looked dirty. Happy, but dirty. When I saw marks on his back much later, he told me they were stretch marks, but the strict house and corporal punishment his father practiced made me think differently.

"One time my dad beat me so bad. He woke up, and there were acorns in his boots. He went out to put his shoes on and yelled as he cut his feet. He called the three of us out of bed to find out who played the trick. We all looked at each other. Dad said, 'One of you better admit it, or you'll all get a whipping.' My brothers both said they didn't do it. Dad looked at me all angry-like, but I hadn't done it. I decided it was better just one of us get a beating instead of all of us. Next day it happened again. Dad came running in, furious with me. I got punished again, this time harder.

"That night," he said, "Dad looked out the window and saw a little squirrel shuttling back and forth putting acorns in his boots. He came in and couldn't believe what I'd done for my brothers."

Conner graduated Valedictorian from his high school class and received a military scholarship to attend college. He credited his teachers and guidance counselors for giving him incentive and catapulting him. His father would make fun of him saying, "Why you studying so much?" and his parents discouraged him from attending college. Neither of his parents were college educated. His mother worked several secretarial jobs, usually at the schools where her sons attended. Conner gladly accepted the free, high-quality education the military would provide. It was his opportunity for a better life, he said, to get beyond the poverty of his childhood. He was living the American Dream, and he was proud of that.

I thought about him after our short time together that evening. He had opened up and shared so freely with me.

Two days after the drive in the Corvette, Conner came to visit me in my cubicle. He stood in the doorway, looking sheepish and sweet.

"D … do you have a VCR?" he stuttered.

"Yeah, I do. Why?" I said flatly.

"Have you've seen *Dumb and Dumber?*" he asked.

"No," I said, face turned, eyebrow raised. I only knew it was a Jim Carrey comedy.

"Well," he stuttered slightly again, "wwwould you like to watch it with me sometime?"

"I guess. Sure," I said.

"Okay, great," he said exhaling. He quickly walked away.

I immediately put my hand over my mouth to muffle my laugh. Sucked my cheeks in and thought about how sweet and embarrassed he just was. I heard him return and sit in the cubicle beyond mine. I was smiling so hard. I'd not been asked out in a while, and he was sweet.

We never did watch *Dumb and Dumber*, thankfully. Thursday night he picked me up at my apartment, a complete gentleman, opening doors, smelling clean with cologne in his dated but neat civilian clothes. We found a quiet table and had dinner along the river. We talked and flirted for hours over dinner and strolled into the evening. He was not smooth, not suave, instead honest, transparent, simple, and lovely.

At the end of our date, he walked me to my door. He asked, "Can I make lunch for you tomorrow? I don't want to wait until dinner to talk to you again."

"Yeah," I said smiling. "Sure, that would be great."

"Okay, well, see you tomorrow at the office." He began to wave, raised his hand and kissed me quickly on the cheek.

"Goodnight, Conner," I said with a warm smile.

"Goodnight."

His unassuming kiss on the cheek was just the way I wanted our first date to end. But I also looked forward to more. A quick-paced love affair ensued. He told me I was beautiful, caressed my face, held my hands, kissed me on the cheek and lips, his full lips sweet with tenderness. We passed each other on the way to the water cooler while at work, smiling and winking, shared lunches at my apartment, dinners out, softball games a few nights a week.

Conner liked that I could be professional, intelligent, and classy at work and athletic and 'one of the guys' on the field after work. He fell in love quickly, as did I.

When I flew home to surprise my sister Elizabeth at her high school graduation, I told my parents, "I think I met the man I'm going to marry." My parents looked at me with surprise.

My mother said, "One life event at a time here, please!" She was smiling and joking, but not really. They knew I was not one to say things like this lightly.

Conner was a sweet, innocent man. He had only dated one girl seriously in high school and during his time in college. That ended slowly with a demanding military schedule. Conner was gentle; he was bright, tall, thin, lovely, blue-eyed. I fell in love with his simplicity. Our relationship was simple, straightforward communications, naked honesty. There was never tension or discomfort; everything was talked about. I'd never bared my emotions and feelings so easily with a man.

We fell onto my bed kissing one afternoon. Kissing him was endless in the beginning. We rolled on the bed, deep hard kissing, licking, touching everywhere. I was on top. I reached to undo his belt, kissing his neck. He pulled away and lay flat on the bed.

"What's the matter?" I ask startled. He stared up at me.

"Is everything okay? Did I hurt you?"

"No, it's not like that," he said.

"Well, what is it? What's wrong?" I sat straddling him.

"I just don't want to do this," he said.

"Okaaaay?"

"I mean, I don't want to have sex."

"I didn't think we were going to have sex today. I was just having fun."

I'd never had a man act this way. Was he insecure about his size? Did he have a scar? His actions were unusual. I moved to lie next to him instead.

Stroking his chest, I said, "I'm sorry if I was rushing you."

"It's not that, I just had another girl try to force me to have sex with her."

"Oh, don't worry I wasn't ready for that either. I just wanted to keep playing. I like this daytime thing!" I said smiling.

I kissed his chest, played my way up to his neck, ears, and lips. He responded. We were back on track.

Until then, I assumed he had sex with his long term high school girl friend. We hadn't talked specifics, but she traveled to see him and vice versa.

"I don't want you to think I'm a prude or anything, I just don't want to be pressured like I was before. And anyway ... " He hesitated. "I haven't had sex, well, intercourse. I don't know if I'll wait until I get married, but I do think it would be kinda nice."

I was surprised. I hadn't had intercourse yet either. I wasn't a bit prudish, but I was protective of my body, waiting for the right man. My virginity was empowering. It was unique, like me. Knowing about his virginity brought me closer to him than I anticipated. I had been living in the city, clubbing, making out, dancing - living a fantastic single city life. Good friends of mine were having sex days or hours after they met people. That didn't work for me. My attraction to Conner's innocence and simplicity increased ten-fold that day.

We grew closer, shared hopes, plans. We talked of helping people through our work, especially the poor around the world. He spoke of honesty, integrity, hard work. Those were all my dreams too. We were together in Texas for six weeks before he went back to school.

I flew to see him again in late summer. When I returned to New York City, a long distance relationship ensued. We emailed several times a day and talked as much as we could. Conner changed all his medical school applications. Instead of focusing on the Midwest and schools close to his parents, he decided to apply on the East Coast close to me. It had only been a few months, but we were making long term decisions and long term plans to be together.

That September, Conner traveled to New York City to visit me and meet my family for the first time. It was an anticipated event, as this was a serious boyfriend and my family was tightly woven. We drove from my apartment in Greenwich Village to my parents' home in Connecticut. He spilled coffee on his old and dated jeans on the drive. A quick stop at the mall, we bought a new pair of pants and a shirt. He didn't have many civilian clothes as it was. He wore his uniform to class and free time was rare, so he didn't need many.

My mother liked him instantly. Conner stuttered when he was nervous. He was respectful of my parents and their home. My mother appreciated his sweet, gentle spirit. His words were tender but direct. We all sat around the sunny kitchen table in the bay window for hours.

Unexpectedly Conner said, "I know it's kind of early, but I was wondering if I could spend Christmas with your family?"

He directed the question to my mother, who then looked to Dad for his reaction. We had not discussed this possibility as a couple and I was surprised he brought it up. It was only September; we'd only met a couple months ago, and Christmas was three months away. My whole family was a little taken aback by his request. We had always spent Christmas as a family, at home both Christmas Eve and Christmas Day. But this was Conner's way. He was direct and honest. He wanted to be with me, and he was falling in love with my family, too. It was all foreign to him, and he wanted it all.

After some uncomfortable glances with my sister, I said, "Conner, this can probably wait."

"Well, actually, it can't wait too much. I need to make travel plans and request leave pretty soon," Conner added shyly.

Everyone was uncomfortable; nobody sure how to respond as it had only ever been the five of us around the fondue table watching *It's a Wonderful Life* on Christmas Eve. My immediate family was so close and so closed. Nobody else had ever belonged in our home at the holidays.

Dad said, "Well, why don't we take a family vote," as he looked around the table. "What does everyone think?" We were all kind of smiling that goofy, uncomfortable, not-sure-what-to-say-trying-to-be-nice smile.

Christine my youngest sister said, "I don't know about anyone else, but it's fine with me."

"And really I think it could work," Mom said. "What do you think, David, Elizabeth?"

"It's okay with me," Elizabeth, my other sister said.

"Yes, Conner, you would be welcome here at Christmas time," Dad said.

This was a significant move and entry for Conner since no one but the five family members had ever been together for

Christmas Eve and Christmas Day. I thought it was considerate of my dad to ask everyone for their input.

But Conner's family had a very different reaction. His parents thought it insulting we would vote in front of Conner like that. They were proud of Conner when they wanted to be. He was not offended, and neither was I. Although I'd not met them, I began to sense I hadn't been given the full story of his family dynamic.

My parents were born and raised in Chicago. My father was an engineer, my mother a high school teacher. They had both earned master's degrees. I too was born in Chicago, and we moved to Connecticut after my father was promoted at his company. I am the oldest of three girls. Our household had high expectations for academic success as well as extracurricular pursuits. All of us were involved in music lessons and among the three of us we played piano, violin, viola, trumpet, saxophone, flute, and clarinet. We were all also athletic, involved in basketball, softball, swimming, diving, biking, and hiking.

We lived on eight wooded acres in Connecticut. It made a fantastic playground and 'learning lab.' We had play forts and schools and two ponds to skate on in the winter time. My parents entertained year round, especially in the summer when friends and families would come play volleyball, horseshoes, basketball, bocce, and swim at our house. It was a happy place to grow up. We were fortunate to have such a wonderful environment to live and thrive.

But the three of us also grew up in a strict, at times rigid, household. We were spanked as children, punished with extra chores and finished our previous night's dinner for breakfast if we hadn't cleaned our plate. Our television time and content was limited. I was not able to watch shows like Family Ties as a kid and always felt left out of the jokes other kids told at school the next day. The two-dollar movies at the Town Hall were always a few months old. Kids in middle school started going in groups or on dates Friday nights. I would make excuses why I was too busy. Even into college my parents questioned my going to an 'R' rated movie.

Lying or dishonesty of any kind was simply not acceptable, early 8am Mass compulsory on Sundays regardless of age or later weekend job responsibilities. And we all had regular household chores and responsibilities. Sometimes these chores had to be done before the 7am high school bus. Our parents never came close to spoiling us. We received gifts at Christmas and on our birthdays and a new outfit and shoes to begin each school year. My parents were savers. They didn't live deep in debt. They worked hard for their money – and spent it wisely. They drove cars for a decade, kept furniture until even Goodwill wouldn't accept it, and rarely ate out. They were conservative, educated people. But any educational needs, opportunities for family exploration, long summer vacations, day trips dubbed 'Mom's Adventures,' or Broadway musicals in New York City were always planned for and provided. Experiences and travel were valued over buying and collecting stuff. My parents provided a well-rounded youth for us. I worked hard to please and impress my parents in my studies, my sports, and frankly in everything I did. I wanted to make them proud of me and proud of my choices.

Conner grew up in a family environment so different from mine. I didn't understand the extent to which that would shape the way we interacted as a couple until years into our relationship because it was so bewildering to me.

I spoke with his mother for the first time soon after Conner and I met. He unexpectedly handed the phone to me.

"Hi!" I drew in air quickly.

"Hi Julie," his mother said, with a slight accent.

I was nervous and quickly joked, "So, tell me all the bad stuff. I've already heard all the good stuff about this guy." Silence on the other end of the phone. Lump in my throat. I didn't want to screw up my first impression, but it might have been too late. "Just kidding, Conner has told me so much about you and Brad. On our first date, he showed me the picture of you two he keeps in his wallet."

"Oh, okay, great," she said slowly. Her voice was timid and quiet. I didn't know how to engage. I didn't expect such a timid voice or lack of interaction given Conner's verbal nature.

"Well, it was nice talking to you." I slowed my cadence a bit and spoke more carefully, thinking maybe she didn't understand me. "I hope you have a good weekend. Let me give you back to Conner."

I first met Deb and Brad a few months later at West Point on a brisk sunny autumn day. Conner's twin brother Jonathan was spending the fall semester studying at West Point as an exchange student. I drove to West Point to meet both his twin and parents.

We all shook hands, exchanging greetings under the ancient trees of West Point. We talked and walked slowly to the Saturday morning parade. It was a little odd dating a twin at first. They looked and moved almost identically, but their mannerisms and personalities were different. I worked to keep the conversation flowing. Unlike in my family, Conner's father was the more verbal of the two parents. I asked about their travels, shared times I had spent with my family at military football games as a kid, asked about their other son, Ben, and their work. I did most of the talking, along with Conner and Jonathan. His parents didn't know much about their sons' lives or the military, and I was surprised. But it was a relaxed, pleasant day. Conner was happy with the way all was progressing, blending all these people together whom he loved.

Conner and his family assumed they would all stay at my parents' house in Connecticut. It was a little over an hour's drive to West Point, and they thought it made perfect sense. They wouldn't spend money on a hotel. At this point, I had never met Conner's parents, nor been to their home, and my parents had only met Conner now on two occasions. No one in my family would have made this sort of assumption and invite themselves to spend the night anywhere, no matter the cost of area hotels. I decided it had been a miscommunication between Conner and his parents, with Conner offering my parents' home to them.

All four of Conner's family spent the night in my parents' home. Deb and Brad had been kind, and I was interested in watching and getting to know another side of Conner through his family. That evening we played pool and ping pong at my parents' home. My parents were most accommodating and wonderful hosts to these people they just met. Conner's father drank quite a bit that evening, especially hard liquor. I used to bartend at a college town bar and continued to offer to make him drinks. At the time, I didn't think anything of his drinking. Maybe he was nervous. I didn't know what an alcoholic looked like, and I just wanted our guests to be happy.

I did notice that night Conner acted differently around his family which bothered me. He was immature, his jokes and language more sophomoric. My parents were doing dishes in the kitchen. They asked me how I thought the weekend was going.

"Great," I said, "except I don't like the way he acts around his family. He's not himself."

I was uncomfortable that evening. In my gut, something was icky.

Conner explained more about his family and his parents' drinking problems after their visit. It sounded like he was working to coddle them through the weekend as they felt out of place. His father had some back problems; he was on disability – I didn't really understand all he was saying. I didn't know anyone on disability. I didn't know anyone who was an alcoholic. But I knew I felt sorry for Conner. He had so much he was juggling. With me, he could be himself. And I could be myself. We would just "get through" the times with his family, he said.

"I barely see them. And you can see they don't even know me anymore."

A military career would take him around the world. I wanted him to be able to lean into my family, get the support and love that was missing from his world, leave the tiring coddling behind. There were times I would hear his father over the phone criticizing him about something. *Why you doing that for, Conner?'* was his favorite question. I wanted to sweep Conner away. He was so smart and full of goodness. He had such potential for more good. I wanted to be a part of that. I wanted us to build upon our goodness together. And I wanted my family to help him flourish with all the love they could give. I wanted to love him forever and share my wonderful life.

I visited Conner's hometown for the first time in December. We had spent the Christmas in Connecticut as a result of the family vote and would spend New Year's in Oklahoma with his family. It was a nice holiday of traveling. We flew into Tulsa, and his father picked us up at the airport. We made small talk in the car. Then I stiffened pulling onto their street. Conner had described his childhood home as "a little country home" that was "cute as a button." He told me it was set on a large farm, and his father raised cows, beautiful fields for kids to run and play. It sounded like a movie set from Little House on the Prairie to me. His description was probably part childhood reminiscing and part wanting to impress. Maybe this was Conner's delusion. Maybe it was my crushed expectation. Maybe it was the beginning of his lying.

We passed some nice, well-kept houses. Then the road turned from bumpy pavement to dirt and I wasn't sure what to expect, but still had an image from his description. When we turned into the long driveway, I felt a lump in my throat. The house ahead was dilapidated. Paint peeled from the siding. The roof was in bad need of repair. Tools lay in the yard. Chain link fence caged several large barking dogs. The front porch was loosely attached to the house. A couple of mangy cows grazed in the distance. We drove around and through potholes on our way up the dirt driveway.

I kept my smile pasted on complimenting the beautiful sunset and the lovely trees in the distance. But I felt sad this was the place Conner spent his childhood. How difficult his life must have been. The stories he told flooded my mind as we drove.

His father was always between jobs, but could fix anything. His mother was sexually harassed by a school principal. A lawsuit followed, and she lost. The alcoholism, whippings, random family members smoking marijuana, church three days a week, Bible verses recited, adultery by both parents, prayer before dinner, his parents would 'nap' on the weekends with their bedroom door locked. Both sets of his grandparents had been through nasty divorces. The more I heard, the more it seemed like a huge mess of dysfunction to me. But in his memory, this place was filled with happiness, or at the least that was what he wanted me to think.

We spent the next few days at the house. While we were there, they had some sewer problems so we couldn't shower every day. His parents were embarrassed, but these things couldn't be predicted. I felt sorry for them. It looked like their bathroom was in the midst of being remodeled, but that it had been a multi-year project. When I offered to cook dinner, I found few cooking utensils and the pots and pans were old and worn. Conner had always talked of eating canned vegetables and frozen dinners as a child. I made a simple chicken stir fry with some canned pineapple, and everyone raved it was simply the best. I felt out of place, but I felt Conner and his twin were out of place too. This was his childhood home, but this was not what he wanted for his home, or for his own family.

New Year's Eve, Conner's parents, his brother and date, and I all went to a hotel party event. Each couple had their own room, but we would spend the evening and midnight at the party. We all sat at a table in a hall at the All You Can Drink event. The evening was fun, although overpriced as all New Year's Eve parties are. Conner's father, Brad, drank way too much and as some drunken men do, he thought he was particularly strong that evening. After much coaxing and pleading he wanted to pick up both Deb and me, one in each arm on the dance floor. Conner and I looked at each other. He said he would be there to catch me. Brad crouched down, and Deb and I got on either side of him. He wrapped his arms around both our legs and stood quickly to show his prizes to the room. As expected, all of us went tumbling to the dance floor. Brad was of course apologetic, but this was typical of the 50-something year old adolescent behavior during the visit. But I had a good time because Conner was there and we danced. I loved him more than anyone. We had a hotel room and a shower that night. I loved sleeping close to him. We weren't having sex but being intimate, sleeping together; all felt right.

Conner would apologize profusely for weeks and months after the New Year's Eve event with his drunken parents. But it was New Year's Eve and lots of people get drunk that night every year. I felt embarrassed for him, but nothing more. We rang in the New Year and were both ecstatic that 1997 would bring us geographically closer together.

One trip out west, we spent the day at the Como Hotel, a classic mountain resort on a lake. We had lunch at the Lake Terrace restaurant to celebrate his medical school acceptance and then we walked the grounds in the afternoon - a spectacular spring day in the mountains. We started talking about marriage. Traditionally several military officers get married the same weekend as college graduation. I didn't want to rush a wedding or complicate his graduation. But I did want to talk about getting married. Conner was ready, and I wanted to wait to get engaged and have time to plan a wedding.

We talked about our married names. I didn't want to change my last name to his. My dad had three daughters and I wanted his name to continue. In social settings, I could be Mrs. Conner, that would be fine, but professionally, Freed was a noble name. A handful of publications had my name already, and I'd always really liked my name. I came from people who have traveled, who have been freed from their trappings. My ancestors came to the US long ago. Growing up we never practiced much of the eastern European traditions. My Polish grandparents intentionally pushed their family to be American. And yet generations later, I am proud of my Polish and German heritage. My teammates growing up used to chant "Freedom!" when I was at the free throw line or up to bat. I was Julie Freed and I was married to my name.

My mother never liked when couples were referred to as Mr. and Mrs. John Smith. It was as if the woman and her names were subsumed. The wife became a 'Mrs' and identity free. I didn't want a boring last name. And I didn't want just to be a 'missus.' I wanted to be a spouse, a partner, a mother, a doctor, but not a missus. I am Julie Freed. That is my name, my identity, my family, me. The cultural tradition of changing last names is one little girls begin thinking about so young. They write their names in elementary script handwriting using a boy's last name they have a crush on. It's a sad pastime reflective of a male dominated society where a girl dreams of being a wife instead of being a woman.

"I love your family, Julie. Maybe I should change my name to yours?" he offered.

"Really?" I was shocked.

"Yeah, I mean we're closer and more a part of your family than mine. Neither of my parents, you know, were the greatest. They did the best they could but … I'd be proud to have your family name."

"Goodness. I don't know what to say, Conner." I hadn't even thought about that as an option. Part of the reason I wanted to keep my name was to maintain my identity. Would changing his name to mine mean losing some of his?

"I want us to share a name. I think that's important," he said.

"I'm not sure it's the right thing to do. I find it completely touching and a wonderful idea, but won't your family be upset?"

"They might at first, but I kinda think it makes sense. My family has three boys. And it's really Grandpa George's name. He left Grandma Barbara to raise her kids alone. I'd just like us, and our family and kids down the road, to all have the same name." He was smiling as he spoke.

"Well, we can do that socially, informally. I don't have to be Dr. Freed taking kids to school and military stuff, but professionally I can be. You think about the name."

"Well, I have."

"I think it would be wonderful, but maybe we need some time to think on that."

δδδδδ

Conner ranked in the top of his graduating class. It was a proud day for him, for me, and for his family. Extended family flew in from the west coast, his family from Oklahoma, and local friends all came to celebrate.

Following the moving graduation ceremony, Conner's parents decided the four of us would go directly to TGI Fridays for dinner. They didn't tell anyone else where we were going or even that we would be eating. We returned to find all the extended family waiting for us and surprised that we had already eaten.

"We thought you were stuck in traffic or something," Jonathan, his twin was annoyed. A somewhat tense conversation followed.

When it came to Conner's family, I let them fight it out. Deb was a quiet woman, and it had been more than whispered that I was already too 'northeast,' too educated, and too rich, so I always tried to go with the flow around his family. Awkwardness and discomfort ended his graduation day, the culmination of four hard years.

Conner moved to Baltimore that summer. We found an apartment he could afford, but it was on the edge of a ghetto. During his first night he said he heard gunshots. The tiny apartment had a huge window, which at first glance, seemed wonderful, but it made for hot, uncomfortable afternoons and evenings. It was a horrible first week for him. He threw up every day of orientation. It hadn't occurred to me this might be alcohol induced. He told me he was worried he'd made the wrong decision to attend this school. He'd grown accustomed to the rigidity, challenging schedule, and physical demands of the military. The social breakfasts and afternoon picnics during orientation seemed soft to him. He started to doubt he would get a quality medical education, even though enrolled in a top rated program. I drove up to bring him food every day, and sometimes spent the nights with him to make sure he was keeping something down.

Days later found him in the throes of rigorous hours of anatomy lab and long lecture hours. I continued my graduate work and assistantship. It felt good to finally be living close to each other. Every weekend we were together and usually drove to meet for dinner on Wednesdays. We loved cooking together, studying at coffee shops and book stores, bike riding, and exploring our new community and state parks. Our closeness and physical intimacy grew. We explored each other more. We learned how to please the other. Without intercourse, it was easier to gauge how giving he was, sexually. The playing, the teasing, the not having sex was hot. We were inseparable, spending the night at each other's apartments, meeting new friends. We were both highly-stimulated, growing professionally and growing more into each other.

7
ROSEMAN BRIDGE

Friday 14 November 1997

The snowstorm was blinding. We had flown from Baltimore into Chicago, rented a car, and driven west. I didn't know to where. Cars were pulled off to the side of the highway.

The day before, Conner told me to pack a weekend bag. He picked me up after class and drove to the Baltimore airport. Something was up if Conner had made all these plans without me knowing. I was excited about the weekend, especially not knowing what to expect. I wanted him to propose. I wanted to be engaged.

I asked him at the airport, "Have you talked to my parents?" I was nervous but excited.

"Mom, we're at the airport and I just found out we're flying to Chicago, but that's all I know. Have you guys talked to Conner?"

"Yes."

"So you know what's going on?" I asked. Prodding, "I assume he is proposing?"

I had inadvertently found out a few weeks ago he was shopping for rings at various dealers in New York City. And we had been talking and agreed that getting married in the summer of 98 would allow us to go on an extended honeymoon. Once he started his medical school rotations, academic summers would no longer exist. We had been dating a little over a year, mostly long distance, but we saw no reason to wait. We were ready to say, "I do."

"He didn't give us any detail, Julie."

"So, what do you know?"

Mom was quiet and mumbled only a cheerful, "Hmm." Her obvious withholding of information only made everything all the more exciting as she was clearly not concerned.

"You and Dad talked to him and said it would be okay for us to get married? I just need to know that before the weekend gets going."

She hesitated. "Yes, Julie he contacted us." The smile came through in her voice. "I'm very excited for you. But I really don't know anything about your flights."

"That makes me feel better. I'll call you with an update as soon as I know more. I'm so excited! Hope you guys have a good weekend too!"

"Have fun, Julie. We love you!" She put my mind at ease.

I was born in Chicago. Maybe we were going someplace fantastic downtown? Despite my incessant prodding, Conner was not giving any indication of our destination.

After a relaxing flight, we got on the road. At various exits, I guessed that was where we were getting off, until we were on I-88 through Naperville. No one I knew lived in this direction. He told me we had a long way to go, and we kept driving. We got caught up during the trip on school stuff and current events. The heavy snow continued. The interstate grew dark. I grew more reflective and concerned, not about marrying Conner, but marrying his family. Knowing that a proposal was imminent, there were lots of things I wanted to get off my chest and hopefully make some agreements, about his family.

"Conner, you know I love you and think the world of you, but I'm really worried about your family."

"Why?"

"Well, when it's just us, everything is wonderful. You are sweet, smart, thoughtful. You are yourself. But when your family is around, you're different. We know they really don't like me or like us together."

My voice became more stressed. I looked from the snowy road illuminated in the headlights to his profile and back again hoping for a response.

"You've told me about their comments about me being 'too educated, too northeast.' I still don't know how either of these are bad things."

"Julie, that's them and not me," he said.

"Yeah, I know that."

He looked at me sweetly, "I'm yours, your one and only … for always."

I stared at him, then sighed and looked back to the falling snow.

"My parents only know me as their little boy growing up, dirty on the farm. They don't know who I am now or what I want in life. They don't even know us. But they are my parents."

"Yeah and that's what worries me. They are your parents and you act differently around them." I cried because this was all painful to articulate and deliver carefully. "And when you talk to them on the phone it's like you twang up the country accent and dumb yourself down. It's like it's not even you. And your twin brother and you argue all the time, on the phone, in person. You two are so competitive about everything, even your girlfriends. I'm not used to all the fighting, questioning, criticizing. It's so tense for me around all of them. And when you're different, it makes it hard for me to navigate. I don't know how to act and what to say to avoid offending someone."

"Oh, honey, I don't know what you mean. Every family has issues from time to time. Even your family has problems. We deal with stuff different in my family. We talk it out; we question each other. I don't really think any of it matters. I know I want to get married. And I want to marry you. I'm ready to make my own life and our own life together."

"I know, I know. And I want that too."

I wiped tears. The windshield wipers and patterns in the driving snow were mesmerizing. I let my eyes relax and dance about the snow designs.

"Do you remember that first time in Connecticut with your parents at Mom and Dad's house?" I asked. "You were not yourself. I remember telling Mom and Dad exactly that in the kitchen. They asked me how I thought the evening was going after dinner. And I told them 'Great, except Conner is weird around his parents, even his laugh. He's just different.' You all were downstairs playing pool and ping pong. I don't know how all that is going to impact us down the road." The tears rolled.

Conner was reassuring and gentle. "Look, they are NOT going to affect us, Julie. We love each other. Everybody in the world can see that. We are going to do whatever we want together with this love we've found. If they can't see that, then they're idiots. And they will miss out on being in our lives. I mean if they don't trust me to make me own decisions ... then ... their loss. There's nothing I can do."

"But what if they don't think you're ready? Like your brother said. He thinks you should wait a year."

"They all didn't want me to go into the military either. And now look at me, soon to be a doctor. They can't always see far down the road. I'm not like that. I know this is right deep in my heart and soul. I've been driving to you all my life."

I cried more at his tenderness and couldn't agree more. I knew apples who had fallen far from the tree. Friends told me stories of their ill family members. He was *not* an alcoholic like his parents. He had seen its destruction. He was academically driven and goal-oriented. He wanted to create a better life than his parents had. He had experienced real love in our relationship, and that's what he wanted to build and grow together.

"My parents don't know me like you do," he reassured me. "And they don't know you like I do. They will understand over time. It might take a couple months. But they will love you someday, too."

"But what if they just don't understand? I can't change that I'm from Connecticut. I can't change that my parents have a nicer house than yours. I can't change that my parents went to college. I don't get it. It all seems like jealousy instead of happiness for you. I mean … it all seems so twisted. I just don't get it! How could parents and family be jealous of their son and brother?" I asked. "They don't get me, Conner."

"Well, they are going to have to. We are going to start *our* life, *our* family now. And we're not even going to see them that much. You know how much I love being with your family. We'll have some holidays and trips here and there. It's going to be okay, Julie. They are my family, and I will make it all work."

"I just hate that they are the only people we know who don't love 'us.' My family loves you, Conner, and so do all of our friends. Nora and Jackie adore you. I wish this was easier."

I didn't know what else to say. I cried quietly, wiping my nose. I was sad for Conner that he had to deal with all of this. When we finally pulled off the snowy highway and into a little motel, I was sad we had to have that conversation, disappointed that our probable engagement weekend was interrupted with difficult conversations about his family. I hoped I hadn't ruined things.

Conner set the alarm for early Saturday morning. It seemed especially early since we had rolled in about midnight. It was a cold winter morning, and everything was brilliant white. We got back on the road and continued driving west. I still had no inkling of where we were going. Conner looked carefully for highway and exit signs and seemed unsure of where to turn off. It wasn't clear if he was looking for breakfast, another highway, or an exit. He refused to allow me to look at a map and help. He told me to close my eyes. I was getting excited and wanted to peek but didn't.

We came off the highway.

"Okay, you can open your eyes," he said. We were atop a small bridge. A snowy creek babbled beneath us. I thought, "This is pretty." I looked at him and smiled.

He said sweetly, "Okay, you have to close your eyes again, honey." Then about a minute later he said slowly, "Okay, you can open them now."

A snow covered road lay ahead of us without tire tracks. And in the short distance a beautiful red covered bridge. It was Roseman Bridge in Winterset, Iowa. The tears started falling as I sat in the car looking about. Conner sat watching me, drinking in my reaction. "I can't believe it, Conner," I cried softly. Putting my hand over my mouth, I whispered, "This is amazing."

Last night's snow had put a quiet blanket over the scene. It made me want to hold my breath. The scene was covered with quiet and surrounded by peace. The snow reminded me of my parents' home in Connecticut. After a heavy snow, everything was hushed. Off the twinkling snow I could almost hear myself whispering as a young girl, from our back deck to the white woods. No school, just sledding, ice skating, hot chocolate. That early morning at the bridge was no different. Everything was blanketed. And Conner and I were the only people on earth.

My head turned slowly as I breathed deeply. My nose filled with fresh crisp air. Panning round, I loved the vast stage Conner had chosen for the proposal of marriage. The small river flowed out to our left; the red bridge roof was shrouded in white. Tears of joy flowed. He had brought me to Roseman Bridge, made famous in James Waller's novel, The Bridges of Madison County. We had read this book together the previous summer when we met, and it was the first movie we watched together.

"Would you care to walk with me to the bridge?" Conner asked demurely.

I could only nod and smile as I cried. We stepped in the virgin snow and walked with hands squeezed together toward the bridge. I had to stop, grab tissues from my winter coat pocket, and wipe my eyes and nose. I was in disbelief.

As I wiped my messy face I told him coyly, "I didn't even remember Roseman Bridge was in Iowa. You know how bad my geography is!" Everyone always says how bad they are at math, and the joke was not lost on Conner.

We walked to the entry and stopped. Conner took both my hands and looked at me through his tear-filled eyes. He said, "This kind of certainty only comes but once in a lifetime."

I smiled and watched as he knelt before me. He was slow and deliberate but also nervous. I wiped my eyes with tissues in one hand, and he took the other with both of his hands.

"Julie, will you marry me?"

I squeezed his hands with my left and my right covered teary eyes as I smiled. I uncovered my face and looked tenderly at him for a minute. "Could you please ask me that again?"

He exhaled and smiled through his own tears. "Will you marry me, Julie?"

"Yes, yes, yes!" I said staring right into his big blue eyes. I bounced on the puffy snow beneath us.

He opened a ring box and a brilliant princess-cut diamond on a platinum band shone up at me. My pressed hands went to my lips.

"Oh, my God, Conner, it's all so perfect! And so are you."

He placed the beautiful ring on my finger. It was a spectacular two carat square cut stone. Squares were my favorite. The perfect shape for a mathematician! We took photos along the bridge and walked through the snow-covered bridge. Couples before us had carved their initials and messages of love all along the inside.

A man in the distance was shoveling a path to his small house. He waved us over. It was his home and also a gift shop. He welcomed us inside. We shared our engagement with this stranger who acted thrilled. We bought some mementoes of our lovely morning and marked the beginning of our lives together with a Christmas ornament.

Emails about our engagement quickly made it around Conner's med school class, friends of mine, and students at the university. I even overheard one girl telling another in a coffee shop on my campus about this engagement that was, "just *so* romantic." Our story had become somewhat of an urban legend, but it was true, and it was wonderful. On Tuesday morning, my class of undergraduates immediately noticed the rock on my finger and begged to hear the whole story.

"We want all the details!" the almost all female class begged and giggled.

Besides being in love and being in love with being engaged, I simply loved the way Conner loved me. No one had ever treated me as sweetly and as tenderly as he did. Looking back, perhaps I was more in love with the way he loved me than I was with him. It's difficult sometimes to separate the love one feels for a person from the love they express and feel for you. But I did know that it was good. Conner made me want to be a better person. My parents had always hoped the same for me. I loved feeling that expectation of betterment and anticipated growth for us both.

We had been dating 18 months, and we wanted to be together, sleep together, have sex, and get married. And we assumed 'us' would be forever. Conner had met almost all my friends during trips to New York City and Connecticut. Everyone adored him, as did I. Not only did my friends adore Conner but several friends confided they wished they had what we had. We seemed so fluid, so well matched. We were very different from one another, but a perfect couple to those around us. And I thought so too.

Not long after our trip to Roseman Bridge Conner pointed out a flaw in the stone he had bought. The stone was cut a bit off, making the top square larger, but the stone not as deep. In addition, if you looked at the stone just right from the side through the prongs, there was a significant visible 'inclusion,' as it's called in the field. It looked like a tiny interior crack in the diamond.

I knew little about diamonds. The military provided an elective short course on diamond purchase. I found this simultaneously humorous and insulting. They didn't teach them how to cook, except in survival training, but they could talk the five Cs of diamond quality. I was happy he knew more than me about this large purchase. The flaws seemed minimal, and I didn't mind it then.

Our engagement was a whirlwind. We toured potential reception locations over Thanksgiving break and set a July 1998 date. My parents planned an engagement party in January, but not before Conner spent Christmas in Oklahoma with his family and me in Connecticut with mine. It would be our final holiday apart. And we originally thought it would be nice to be with our respective families rather than splitting the time and traveling.

Unfortunately, he spent the holiday defending his decision to marry me. His twin brother tried desperately to get Conner to wait a year for marriage. His parents, Brad and Debbie, didn't want him to marry me at all. We had planned to get married in the Catholic Church in my hometown and his mother attacked Conner with statements 'proving' the Pope was the devil. I didn't read the one pager she printed out from the web and mailed to him, but apparently it was "evidence" enough that he should simply not get married in the Catholic Church. It was all ridiculous and yet so painful.

The divide continued to grow between me and his parents. He let me listen in on the conversations he had with them. Conner would stand his ground and tell his family how happy he was, and chronicle all the fun times we had together. He begged them to be part of his new-found joy with me. But they were unrelenting and sadly only one of his brothers would attend the engagement party at my parents' home.

Over the next few months, his parents, more so than his brothers, hammered Conner during every phone conversation as well as in written letters. I was too educated, too 'northeast,' too snobby, too rich, too everything. He would be in the military and shouldn't be married at all, period. It would be too difficult to have a spouse and be moving all the time.

Conner was his mother's favorite, the most sensitive and tender of her three boys. Debbie, sadly, was not a tender or warm person herself. Trying to have a conversation with her was challenging, even for Conner. She was self-absorbed. If the conversation wasn't about Debbie and her marathon training or injuries from her marathon training, not much else interested her. She would sit silently on the other side of a conversation. It was difficult to read her emotions and would prove most difficult for Conner.

Conner decided to give his parents one last chance a month before our July wedding. He traveled out to Oklahoma and spent the weekend trying to convince them of his decision and begged them to support him. They refused. He ended up cutting his trip short because of emotional exhaustion. He had tried everything and had finally given up after months of begging. I couldn't blame him. We would soon be married, and he would become my husband. He would have to emotionally separate himself in some ways from his family if they would not support this life-changing decision. But the pulls and pressure from his brothers and parents would continue long after our wedding day.

At the time, it was a near perfect love story and our future as doctor and doctor, healing and educating, was hope-filled. Together we would make a difference that would live beyond our mortal existence. How fitting when the first home we bought together was on 'Bridal Lane.'

8
MY HOUSE

In Jim's car, our heads swiveled. We needed to get back to Bridal Lane. So much to see and process, more to choke back, so much that was foreign. Decking, a boat, a chair, a picture frame, a table, a milk gallon, a refrigerator, all floated beside the road. Above us curtains, bedding, scraps of clothing twisted and wrapped around every tree. Profound shock and sadness struck my heart which beat hard within my chest. My mouth hung open.

So much lost and misplaced. A neighborhood rearranged and mangled. Instead of homes, boats, and gardens to our right, water whipped and flooded a ravaged structure. What did that house look like before? I saw some pieces of decking floating in the rushing water. Was that from a house near mine? A picture frame floated by, a screen door, a vase, another bar stool, large sections of roofing, a basketball. Lives carried away by the churning sea.

I feared continuing further south. What if our car became stuck or flooded on this bridge? We'd already seen total destruction of human life and home, was there more? As we crossed the bridge that spanned Paix Bayou, I looked far in the distance to the west.

I wouldn't need a house key.

My house was gone.

PART 2

Storm Tracking

The universe, I'd learned, was never, ever kidding.
It would take whatever it wanted and it would never give it back.

CHERYL STRAYED

Wild: From Lost to Found on the Pacific Crest Trail

9
THIS TYPE OF CERTAINTY

Friday evening of our wedding weekend his parents pulled into the church parking lot right after we did. I hadn't spoken with them in months. I knew all they had been saying and writing to Conner about me.

> *Julie was raised in the Catholic church. She's going to make you get baptized Catholic!*
> *She doesn't want to be a housewife, she wants to be a professor! Who's going to take care of you?*
> *Her family is a bunch of northeast snobs. What do they know about you?*
> *She's not even going to change her name. She's a crazy feminist, Conner!*

He shared their painful letters and calls so I might better understand the family dynamics. They didn't understand him. I didn't understand them. He just wanted to get an education and help people through medicine. They thought money was his object of desire. They didn't get him; they didn't get us. We decided to both keep our names legally so as not to make matters worse with his family by changing his name to Freed. Socially we would be whatever people called us. It was painful for us both and the walls of explanation too hard to climb. It was like speaking a foreign language on Mars.

In the church parking lot, the first thing Debbie said was, "So, Julie, are you nervous?"

I thought deeply. I wanted to marry Conner. I wanted him to be my husband. If we messed up our vows or stuttered here or there, so what? Yes, we wanted to be married. We were not nervous about being married. The only thing we *were* nervous about was how she and Brad might behave at our wedding.

I responded probably somewhat curtly, "Nope, not one bit," smiling as politely as I could and turned to walk into the church.

Later we were told, Debbie thought I was rude. My comment was the reason she got drunk at our wedding and why his parents made a memorable scene. So horrible, in fact, that years later friends were still asking me and my family, "How are things going with Conner's parents?"

It was an unusually cool day for late July; a perfect, clear Saturday for a wedding, and even better since I would be wearing a long sleeved dress. My virginity was important to me and I wanted to be covered in white on my wedding day.

Saturday 25 July 1998

In the morning my sisters and I had our hair done. We wanted a small and simple wedding party. My father picked up our bouquets, and the programs had already been delivered to the church. Conner's pencil drawing of Roseman Bridge was the cover of our program. Everything had been finalized, and it was a wonderful morning of anticipation at my parents' home. I was not nervous about getting married. Now that we had seen Deb and Brad at the rehearsal and rehearsal dinner, the initial meeting was behind me and the day was ahead to enjoy.

Realizing our brand new shoes were a little slippery, Christine said,

"Let's go out and scuff up our shoes a bit. We don't want to be sliding down the aisle!" The three of us walked on the black topped area outside the garage, carefully scratched the bottoms of our shoes. We were in shorts and tee shirts, our hair all formal in 'up-dos,' manicured nails, high heeled black shoes for them, white for me. Dad heard all the commotion and laughing from the three of us as we headed out.

He followed, and asked, "Wanna shoot some hoops?" He was carrying a basketball out to us.

"Sure, why not?" I yelled.

Mom followed outside shortly with her camera. We all shot some baskets and laughed heartily at how much this was like the *Father of the Bride* movie we loved. Mom captured it all on film.

The photographer and videographer arrived at the house and began shooting. It took a while to get comfortable with the sudden fame and feel relaxed in front of the camera. Mid-afternoon, the classic Cadillac limo arrived. Elizabeth, Christine, and I loaded into the car and were driven to St. Jude Catholic Church.

All was as I imagined. Pews were lined with candelabras, the altar covered with white urns of flowers, a trumpet played as almost two hundred people entered and were seated. The afternoon sun filtered through the stained glass and lit the church in a classically soft, romantic way.

My parents joined the three of us in the back of the church, and the procession began. My tall, gorgeous sisters in long black gowns processed up the long aisle. My parents held each of my arms as we three walked slowly toward the altar. I could not stop smiling looking from one face to another around the church thinking, "All of my friends and family are here! For us!" I was so lucky to have my loved ones supporting my marriage to Conner. We had arranged to have people seated on both sides of the aisle regardless of their affiliation since Conner and his family had so few friends in attendance.

I finally made eye contact with Conner toward the front of the church. He was beaming as was his twin who stood in support by his side on the altar. We had made it. And this was our moment.

The ceremony was intimate and personal. Conner and I said a couples' prayer to share an extension of our vows. We each said a part – and then spoke together. He broke down during the prayer. I know this was partially due to the stress brought on by his family. He had spent the night before with them, and I'm sure his heart was heavy. Fortunately the priest agreed not to include, "If anyone thinks this man and woman should not be married ... " We didn't want to give his parents any opportunity even for a throat clearing. We lit our own unity candle as well, instead of having our mothers do it.

We exchanged vows and slowly placed our wedding bands on the other's finger. Our rings were engraved with a quote from the Bridges of Madison County book. My ring said, "This type of certainty ... " and his " ... comes but once in a lifetime." The quote was Conner's idea as a reminder of the bridge where he proposed. He was a hopeless romantic and made an effort to create romance in our everyday lives. We were both so certain this would be a love for a lifetime.

We walked down the aisle together husband and wife after a long slow kiss in the afternoon light. We received our guests at the back of the church along with both of our families. I hadn't noticed until then that Debbie, Conner's mother, was wearing a white dress. Didn't she know the unwritten rules and etiquette? Everyone knew this. Conner was embarrassed she was wearing white. But this was Debbie's way of trying to steal attention. Maybe she had to feel like her son still loved her too. She often did this during family events, pulling Conner aside to have private talks with him in the middle of a party or public event. It was, I guess, her way of feeling important or needed.

In the receiving line, Brad and Debbie had the chance to meet some of Conner's new friends and family. They appeared overwhelmed and out of place. They were not social people and were definitely taken back by all the comments. "Conner is marrying into an amazing family." "Julie is such a catch." Joking, "I wish she had married my son!" "You're so lucky to be part of this giving family." But this, unfortunately, didn't seem to set a familial tone for the evening reception or the photography session to follow.

Avenall Pasture, a historical field in the center of town was established in the early 1700s. Wild heather, ancient willow and pine trees framed a large pond. It was often the choice for wedding photographs. During one photo with Conner's family, the photographer placed Debbie and I together in the middle, flanked with all the men from his side. Debbie wouldn't put her arm around me. I took her around the waist, pulled her closer, and said, "Come on Deb, we're family now!" in as cheery a voice as I could manage. Even the photographer said, "Okay, smile. We love each other!" My pasted-on smile in the photograph was proof of the awkwardness of all our interactions with them that weekend.

Back in the limo, Conner and I were relieved that the wedding ceremony went smoothly. Nobody in his family made any major *faux pas*. We could relax. It was time to eat, dance, and thank all the guests who had been so generous. His military friends hooted we would have sex on the drive to the reception, but why rush at that point? We had a wonderfully quiet drive in peace, just us, for about 20 minutes. We held our left hands together, looked at our rings, smiling. I petted his face. He rubbed my thigh through my dress. We kissed and kissed all over each other's faces. It was all light and all sunny. We were finally relaxed. We were married. And we were Mr. and Mrs. Something Different.

We arrived at the hotel and reception. Fortunately the bridal party had a room to themselves to freshen up and eat a bit before being announced. The videographer filmed a fake closing with us leaving on our honeymoon. Meanwhile, guests were welcomed by a harpist during the cocktail hour in a cascading rock garden lit with white lights and candles. Gardens bordered the glass wall of the reception room. It was a starry summer night and elegant wedding reception.

We were finally announced and danced our first dance. No one else was in the room until Conner dipped me in the end with a kiss to standing applause. It was sheer joy for us both. We felt like movie stars in the happiest movie ever made. We 'complained' the next morning that our faces hurt from all the smiling.

Conner's twin gave a wonderful toast, but I later learned that Conner asked him to edit most of it earlier in the day because of odd comments about women in it. I would never have guessed. Jonathan spoke with conviction, clarity, and most importantly love. He would support us and our relationship always; he promised. His words were exceptionally meaningful given his family climate and coolness toward me.

Several friends of ours began dating after meeting at our wedding. One couple, a friend of mine from high school and one of Conner's from the military, met that night and married a few months later. It was rumored a college friend was making out on the golf course with a friend from high school later in the evening. The wedding guests closed down the hotel bar late that night. It was a loved-filled event.

But despite all the joy in the air, Deb was drunk. So drunk she spent a chunk of the evening crying in the bathroom. Guests were talking about it. One of Mom's friends, an outspoken transplanted New Yorker with a thick Brooklyn accent, decided she needed to talk to Deb in the bathroom, crying at the sink.

"You need to clean this up," she said directly, looking her up and down. "You are making a scene and an utter fool of yourself. Please get a handle. This is not about you, this is about Conner and Julie. It's a gorgeous wedding. Clean up and have a good time, okay?"

Deb was reported to have responded well, dried her eyes, and left the bathroom. Shortly after, she reappeared at the reception in a dark mini skirt and tight shirt. She had changed out of her white mother-of-the-groom dress. The new outfit was something you might see on a 20-something in a bar. It was not wedding attire for a 50-something.

Conner and I had been visiting with guests in the garden when we both turned to see Deb wearing her new outfit. A friend told me both our faces dropped.

We looked at each other, and I said to Conner through a forced smile, "What is your mother wearing?"

"I have no idea," he responded through a pasted smile.

He walked calmly over to her, put his arm around her, and asked gently why she had changed. She replied that she "wanted to be comfy for dancing and partying."

And we did party. The eight piece band had our reception going until well after midnight. The band played anything and everything. And the event coordinator commented that the alcohol consumption that night was higher than most weddings.

Conner was embarrassed by his parents. At the end of the evening, he hugged my parents privately in tears before we went up to the honeymoon suite. He thanked them for being so "supportive and understanding through the weekend and ... through everything." My mother and he exchanged a tearful private conversation. They truly loved one another, and he was the son she never had. She loved hearing 'Mom' in a male voice. Our wedding was a wonderful occasion for everyone but Conner's parents. Conner had to struggle to shut them and their behavior out of his mind.

Conner cried hard that evening once we were alone. He was emotionally drained. But afterwards, there was no awkwardness or discomfort. We were ready to be together and once the hundred tiny buttons down the back of my dress were undone - our union was official time and time again. We knew each other. We knew what we wanted. After the tears of hurt, joy, relief, and endless love were shared, we devoured each other. We were one, pleasing the one, nurturing the one, being with the forever one, with rose petals surrounding us.

The following morning at the wedding brunch, none of Conner's family was present. His mother eventually came down but by this time there was no room at our table. We saw his brother again before we left for our honeymoon, and he clearly had spent the evening post-reception drinking, as well. Although almost a dream, Conner was relieved to have the wedding behind him. He wouldn't have to worry about his family again. His new life with me was set to begin.

The good news was when Conner's twin got married years later he learned from our wedding and avoided the pitfalls. Jonathan picked out a long navy blue dress for his mother, made sure the bartenders made weak drinks for his parents, and warned Brad and Deb that if there were any problems, he would not hesitate to have them removed from the reception. Although identical in looks, Jonathan was most definitely more concise and demanding in his manner and way of being. His wedding went off without a hitch.

We returned from our three-week honeymoon to an apology letter from Conner's father. Not exactly an apology letter, but an explanation for their actions during our wedding weekend. Brad explained that Debbie had been really hurt by my comment in the church parking lot. So hurt, she started taking her antidepressants. The medication, he claimed, had made her sensitive to alcohol. Even Conner didn't buy the story. Neither of us wanted to deal with his family yet. We'd had a three week honeymoon to Nova Scotia and Prince Edward Island, but fall classes would be starting shortly for us both and a relationship with Conner's parents would take significant time and patience to nurture. We would have a lifetime to work on it.

10
OUR HOMES

Our first place was a little townhouse between our two campuses in Maryland. We visited my family often in Connecticut. And we drove up and spent a fall weekend in New York City. Nora had just rented a great new apartment on the Upper East Side. She and Alessandro made us a perfect Italian dinner of homemade *gnocchi*. We toasted their new place with delicious Italian reds. And after dinner we all went out to a neighborhood bar and met up with some college friends of mine who also lived in the city. We all sat close together on couches in the front window seats. I was relaxed and comfortable on the cool autumn night warmed by the Italian dinner, sharing an overview of my master's thesis on the Schrodinger equation and next steps.

Conner laughed suddenly and loudly. I thought he had seen something outside or elsewhere in the bar. I quickly ended my conversation, looked to Conner.

"What did we miss?"

He didn't say anything, and the conversation moved to Nora and Alessandro's new uptown place. Conner went to the bathroom. We all swapped work stories and adventures in graduate and business school. At least 15 minutes passed.

One of my friends from university asked, "Where did Conner go?"

"Oh, he's probably just in the bathroom."

"Well, I need to go. Hopefully it's a two-seater," he guffawed.

He returned and reported Conner wasn't in the bathroom. We looked around a bit perplexed. I walked to the back of the restaurant and asked the bartender if there was another door I missed, thinking maybe Conner went out to have a cigar or something. But there wasn't, and we hadn't seen him walk out the front door as we sat in the window seat table. I checked outside to be sure. I walked back to the bathrooms again and couldn't open the women's bathroom door. It was locked, but it had two stalls in it.

I knocked and whispered, "Conner? Conner? Are you in there?"

I thought I heard his voice. This was a joke. He had locked himself in the women's bathroom? I walked a few steps back to the bartender and joked with him. My lips were pursed, cheeks slightly sucked in.

"I'm newly married. And you're a man. Do you think it's a bad sign?" I mocked. "If your husband locks himself in the women's bathroom?"

We were both laughing. I walked the few steps and again tried to talk with Conner through the women's bathroom door. I was laughing while telling him to come unlock the door hoping this joke at my expense would end quickly.

As I waited I said, "Uhhmm honey, this is NOT the men's room!"

I barely heard him say, "I can't reach it."

I was worried. Maybe he was hurt? He couldn't reach the door knob. I asked the bartender if he had a key to the bathroom which he produced immediately. I walked in, and there was Conner on the floor vomiting into the small waste can under a pedestal sink. He was sprawled on a public bathroom floor in New York City.

"Oh, my God," I said. "What's wrong?"

"I'm fine. I'm just really sick. I don't even want you to see me right now."

I patted his back. "It's okay, honey. Do you want some water? Is there anything I can do?"

"No, just leave me here. I can't move anyway. I'll get up when I can. Really, I'm just fine."

"But, Conner, you're in the women's bathroom which makes this extra ... not good. AND you locked the door. AND you've been in here a long time." No response. "You at least need to move to the men's room."

"Okay. Gimme a minute. I'll be fine. Just go back to your friends."

I insisted. I got him into the men's bathroom.

"Really, I'm fine," he said sounding annoyed. "Leave me here and don't make a scene."

"Alright, I'll go back to the table." He waved as I added, "I'll come check on you soon."

"That's fine."

"And no locking doors!" I told him smiling and smirking with the bartender as I closed the door. I gave the key back to the bartender after straightening up the other bathroom.

Less than 10 minutes later, Conner walked quickly out the front door and squatted down on the sidewalk just past our window. His sudden exit abruptly ended our conversation and unfortunately our evening. I apologized and said goodbye to my friends. On our short walk home with Nora and Alessandro, I saw Conner was staggering. For the first time, I realized Conner was drunk. Now I was angry.

"This is what you get for finishing my wine glasses at dinner. I had to keep refilling my glass because you were drinking your wine and then MY wine when I got up to help."

He was a complete mess and nothing productive could come from a conversation. We got him back to their new apartment. I was apologizing and hugging Nora goodnight in her kitchen as Conner lay on the living room floor.

"He hasn't really slept much this week with school and then traveling up here for the weekend. I'm so sorry." The excuses continued, "He probably didn't eat enough today, and he's not used to drinking wine, especially delicious Italian wines." I explained smiling.

We were both giggling and crying.

"It's okay, Jules. Don't worry about it."

"Nora," I paused with eyebrows raised. "He locked himself in the *women's* bathroom!" We lean away from our hug to look at each other, and I say, "What a man, huh?"

Both of us laughed.

"I wish we didn't have to cut things short with everybody and especially you guys tonight."

"There'll be more nights, don't worry about it! We need sleep anyway!" she said.

"Alright, I better get to my patient and make sure he drinks some water before he passes out."

We spent the night in Nora and Alessandro's living room. I massaged his back and put cold cloths on his neck. He vomited all night into one of their kitchen bowls.

δδδδδ

The next few years we were both in school. Christine, my youngest sister, decided to attend the University of Maryland as an undergraduate. It was nice to have family with me there. We would meet for coffee weekly, and she would come to our place for dinner. Conner and I also made regular trips to Manhattan for plays and dinners, day trips to Philadelphia, and Washington DC. It was a great location, and we never ran out of activities, places to explore, and friends to visit.

We both did well in school. And despite our different academic demands and schedules, we spent quite a bit of time together. Conner was in a medical class of 250 students. I was pursuing a doctorate with a handful of other graduate students, but, as is the case for most doctoral students, the research was unique, and work could be lonely. I used to joke with Conner that at least we knew for *sure* he was going to graduate. He was passing the classes, working hard in the clinical rotations. His tasks were well-defined, but I could easily slip through the cracks and end up ABD (all, but dissertation) like many do each year. His work was clearly more physically demanding while mine was much more self-driven and self-motivated - each proved challenging.

Periodically, issues with his family reared their ugly heads. I never looked forward to their visits. Awkwardness and arguments between Conner and his father or his twin were inevitable. Late night conversations with beers in hand rarely ended well. His parents soon announced their divorce. I wasn't really surprised as they had both cheated on each other when Conner was in high school and clearly had financial, emotional, and addiction problems. It was difficult for Conner. He spent hours fielding phone calls from his mother trying to comfort her and move her through the process. Conner's father was curt and cruel. I began to like him even less.

In the meantime, we needed to start thinking about post medical school military assignments. As we approached his fourth year of medical school, we began discussing options for residency. He originally wanted to be a small town family practice doctor. But, like many medical students, his eventual choice of specialty would result from multiple experiences and conversations with professionals in the field. He eventually decided on surgery. It was physically and academically challenging, and he felt he would really be making a tangible difference with each and every patient. I fully supported his choice, even though it would require more time in the military and even longer living far from my family.

College education provided by the military required five years of service, medical school tuition required four additional years, and medical residency would not count toward the nine years of 'payback time.' Surgery required a five year residency, so this meant 14 years in the military. Conner and I had agreed after our military service, we would move to a location of my choice. This would most likely be near family and a high-quality university for me and our future children.

Our 'options' for his medical training were in Ohio, California, Texas, and Mississippi. Of the choices, Ohio seemed the best. I would have universities nearby, and we would be semi-close to my family. During his Mississippi rotation, Conner raved about the coastal location, cost of living, nightlife, and climate. I flew down and was surprised by the beauty of the location.

I had originally chuckled with Conner, "Are there universities in Mississippi?" The state's history was one of racial turmoil, as were many southern states after 'The Great War' or 'The War of Northern Aggression' as Southerners joke. Mississippi's image and economy had been further damaged by movies like *Mississippi Burning* and *The Ghosts of Mississippi*. And the state flag contains a small confederate battle flag. Some view the confederate or rebel flag as one of independence, rebellion, and Southern pride while, for others, it signifies oppression and racism.

Regardless, this is the state's history and it cannot be overlooked or downplayed. For me, it made it an interesting and eclectic place, more diverse than my roots in Connecticut both ethnically and financially. The remarkable past in the state also makes it a home to story-tellers. Every story has many sides and fortunately, for African-American victims, their families, and for justice's sake, the truth is still being revealed today in the Mississippi courts for heinous hate crimes committed long ago.

The coast of Mississippi was a fairly liberal location. The population was made up mostly of Asians, Blacks, and Whites. The Asian population surprised me, until I learned the Gulf Coast became home to many Vietnamese escaping after the fall of Siagon. Some fled Vietnam in their own fishing boats and brought their families to Biloxi, Mississippi, once called the 'Seafood Capitol of the World.' The casino, travel, and entertainment industries drew people from all walks of life. It was a location where I would feel I was on vacation, with the warm sun and palm trees and could enjoy the water, beaches, seafood, history, and southern culture. And it was a place where my research and programs in the public schools could make a difference.

During my visit, Conner and I enjoyed dinner at a little place called Bayside Seafood on the Water. It was a restaurant on a large bayou, under a bridge that overlooked serene marsh grasses. We enjoyed a seafood dinner watching the sunset light scatter about the grasses and the bayou welcoming boats home from their day out at sea.

After my visit, Conner made it clear to the program director that this was the place where he wanted to train. He began shopping for houses with a realtor. They found a waterfront house in a sweet little town. It was expensive for our budget, but Conner was convinced I would love it. He called me in Maryland to tell me he had put a bid on the house.

"You did what?"

"I put a bid on a house."

"Are you sure about this?"

The bid was significantly *under* the seller's asking price and significantly *over* our anticipated mortgage. I made arrangements almost immediately to fly down so we could see the house together. Not only was the house on the water, it was on the same bayou we had enjoyed overlooking during our dinner at Bayside, Paix Bayou. I loved it. The view upon entrance was straight through to the water. It was mesmerizing, and we prayed the seller would accept.

The house was built by the current owner in 1969 after Hurricane Camille destroyed the entire Mississippi coast. He was an electrical engineer and the house was solid. He and his wife lived there without children and pets. The place was immaculate, but dated. Carpet was where there should be no carpet; white Berber carpet covered the kitchen floor.

"They must have eaten out a lot!" I told the realtor.

There was also carpeting in the bathrooms, which was gross. But the walls were freshly painted white, the carpets, although a bit plush and dated, were in good condition. The kitchen had decent appliances, the landscape and lawn were well kept. Best of all was the sunroom. It ran the width of the house along the back, providing wide views of the live oaks watching over the marsh and bayou. I knew that would be my favorite place to sit and be.

We closed the following month. We struggled to pay rent on our townhouse in Maryland and a mortgage on our future Mississippi home that spring. I began interviewing at area institutions and was offered a tenure track position at the university. Our professional lives and paths were meshing.

Conner began his residency the summer of 2001. I never became used to the 100+ hour work weeks. It was inconceivable that residents worked these many hours. And until you've lived it, it's difficult to imagine. A 'day off' for Conner during his first year would be a Saturday when he only had to work from 5am to noon. A surgeon's notion of 'time off' was completely different from the rest of the world. No shifts, only patients in need of care and repair. And there were patients in need every day, hour, and holiday. Pursuing medicine, and surgery in particular, was a grueling task requiring an unbelievable commitment and sacrifice from the physician and their families. The residents mocked their hourly rate of pay and tried not to think about it too much.

Meanwhile, I was getting settled into my new position. Some articles from my dissertation were published, and I began several new research projects. The university provided some funding to build a research agenda, and I was thrilled finally to be a part of the real workforce. Up until now I had essentially been a student my entire life. In my second year, I earned a large grant from the National Science Foundation for promising junior faculty members. The prestige of that grant was better than the money itself, as it was highly selective and noted. The university rewarded me for this achievement. With publications, conference presentations, and a large grant, I was on a fast track to tenure.

While I was receiving lots of accolades for my work and successes, Conner's situation was much the opposite. Although his board scores were high, and he was doing exceptionally well in the residency, it was not the type of professional community that often patted its members on the back. More accurately, residents got kicked in the teeth on a daily basis. Time to enjoy the small successes achieved each day was unavailable, as the next challenge was already in the operating room.

I was climbing my ladder, feeling rewarded for my accomplishments both locally and nationally, while Conner, even though a 'doctor,' was still in training. The competition and criticism in surgery could be severe. Looking back, I don't think

Conner liked that I was 'moving ahead' of him, professionally and financially. It would only be short-lived as he would soon complete his residency. Nevertheless, some underlying jealousy and destructive competitiveness were brewing. His parents continued to accuse me of being too academic and too smart. My success in his eyes might only have served to remind him of that.

As we were enjoying the coastal lifestyle and our living conditions, Conner volunteered to do a year of laboratory research. This would give us another year in Mississippi, another year to pay the mortgage, and another year for me toward tenure. Conner did some interesting studies during this year and I was able to help review some of his protocols and prepare conference presentations. It was a nice year because his hours were not as demanding. Conner wanted to have a baby during his research year, but I felt I had just begun my new job and didn't want to show up with a baby bump in a few months. Once I got a few more lines on my curriculum vitae, maybe I would be ready.

After his research year, he was back in the 100+ hours per week of surgery residency. It was difficult for him as he was now a year behind his original cohorts, mixing with the new cohorts. During his time off, it became increasingly difficult for him to decompress. He was restless. He wanted to have plans, to be running and doing, going to movies and shows. I wanted to enjoy our home, the water, and entertain friends on Bridal Lane. We rode bikes along the beach, made three-course dinners for colleagues, sipped wine on the patio, did day trips to New Orleans and Dauphin Island, went to shows at the casinos, but still the restlessness. He wanted more.

He started buying classic cars to fix them up and sell them or keep them. I was happy he had a hobby and one he could do at home. He bought a Buick Wildcat convertible for my dad. Dad had a Wildcat when he was single. He bought a '57 Cadillac, and then another Cadillac, then another. I couldn't keep up. He would tell me he had bid on something on eBay or was going to see a car in Port City he had found on Craigslist. He would buy them and fix them up with the hope of selling them for more than he spent. Sometimes he earned a little, more often he lost a bit. We had cars in the garage, cars in storage. The cars and the chunks of money out the door stressed our finances and our marriage that year.

Over time he started wanting more sex, more than I wanted. I thought he was stressed. He said it relaxed him; he needed it. He needed it like he needed food he would say. Sometimes he would want sex in the morning and at night for days in a row. It must have been his work I told myself.

One time I said exhausted and irritated, "We just had sex this morning and twice yesterday. I'm just not in the mood!"

"That's like saying we ate breakfast. I'm still hungry for dinner."

I worried about his need for sex not only because I didn't want to accommodate his needs, but it seemed out of the normal range. Sex three to four times a week was plenty for me and from what I read well over the average married couple. I began to keep a calendar so we could talk about it more concretely, since the way he always remembered it was, "We haven't had sex in so long."

It helped our conversations, but not his need. He started masturbating regularly which bothered me, but I really couldn't offer any more of myself.

He started running in the mornings or evenings. He would run a hard and fast ten miles. When he ran he was less restless. He wanted less sex. We were both happier and more content. I tried to help him find peace and grounding that seemed to be missing in his world. He was not reading the Bible or going to church anymore and maybe he had lost some stability. I felt sorry for Conner. Growing up, I was never as connected to religion or the Bible like he was. The Bible had given him direction as a boy. It had given him rules and boundaries. Without that rigid guidance and the intense demands of a residency, he was wound up. He couldn't relax.

I saw some of the paintings and drawings Conner did as a kid. They still hung in his bedroom at what was now his Dad's house. He'd talked of how much he enjoyed art and painting. For his birthday, I purchased a semi-professional starter kit, easel, paints, brushes, and books. We set up the easel in the corner of the sunroom. It was a beautiful place to paint and be in the moment. When Conner painted, he was at peace.

Up until this point I felt quite fulfilled in life. My career was challenging; I loved reading and mental gymnastics, I had a five year federally funded project underway, we had lots of new friends in the area with and without children, and I hadn't felt the maternal instinct clawing yet. When I was younger, long before I met Conner, I wanted to have lots of children. But then reality sank in, career aspirations took hold, and the emotional and financial commitment required to be a parent felt overwhelming. It is an incredible responsibility and not one I wanted to pursue until I was completely ready. With Conner's demanding schedule, I knew most, if not *all*, of the care giving would come from me.

But then, I turned 30 late in July 2003. I felt really comfortable with where I was in life, married, house, good job, and began thinking about that nasty biological clock. My mother had some infertility problems after 30, and I started to think it could take us years to get pregnant, which could put me at 35 with my first child. We talked. Conner had been ready for over a year, so I knew this would not take much discussion. I went off the pill. We used condoms for the next few months as a grace period and began trying three months later.

11
INSTINCT

25 October 2003

I was awoken from a sound sleep at 2am. I felt a little weird burst in my abdomen on the left side. I'd always been able to feel ovulation each month and knew which side was releasing the egg. This was where I felt the mini burst. It was not painful or even uncomfortable like ovulation could sometimes be. This was different from anything I'd ever felt and knew I must be pregnant! I told Conner first thing in the morning. I was elated. He knew I had always been able to feel ovulation but of course as a physician was skeptical. I waited a few days to take the test. I sat down with Conner in the living room when he got home from work and told him.

"We're on the nest!"

We had worked through some issues we had with Conner's family and had gone to a counselor. We decided we would renew our vows and begin a family. Conner had even made plans to renew our commitment on a covered bridge in Alabama as a reminder and symbol of the original promise we made at our engagement.

After word of the pregnancy, I became ultra conservative about the foods I ate – no soft cheese or sushi – exposure to any second-hand smoke, the soaps and cleansers I used in the house, et cetera. It was a time of preparation and excitement. In the meantime, we would have to make room for this new little addition to our lives. We already had a three-bedroom home, but one room was my home office. I did not want to convert it to a nursery, physically or symbolically, and another was a guest room for mostly my family members and friends. Another room would really be nice. Then my family could visit, I could still work comfortably and efficiently from home, and we could expand for our growing family.

My dad and I designed a master bed and bath addition. We would add a room over the garage and provide spectacular views of the water. French doors would open from the master suite onto a small deck, and a spiral staircase would lead to a breezy, 360-degree view of both the bayou and the Gulf of Mexico. The new baby could move into the existing master bedroom which was off the kitchen, and it would serve as a playroom and later bedroom for our new little one.

The pregnancy was an incredible time for me. I loved being pregnant. I was getting unbelievably attached to the new life growing and developing inside of me. I was in awe of what the female body was capable of doing. I began to put on weight and it was the happiest time in my life. I'd given up my beloved morning cappuccino in favor of fruit juices made with my new juicer, and felt healthier than ever.

Yoga, pregnancy aerobics, and walking all became part of my regimen. I continued teaching, writing, and doing research. It was a productive time for me academically, and emotionally I felt empowered as a woman. My uterus contained a new life, one that soon produced a palpable heartbeat. I started reading children's books to the growing fetus. The Dr. Sears pregnancy and baby books became my nightly reading. I also took up the cello. I had always wanted to play the cello. I grew up playing violin and viola but now playing an instrument right to my baby with the sound reverberating so close to the growing life was a relaxing, yet challenging, endeavor. I enjoyed playing music to my baby and hoped the future would hold the love of music. All the ultrasounds were going well, work was progressing, construction had begun on the house addition. Conner loved my changing body, sex was great, and I was feeling better than ever.

But, for the first time in our relationship, Conner and I started splitting some of our off-time. He started going out every other Friday night with the guys from work. Every other Friday is what is called a 'Down Friday' in the military. They work eight ten-hour shifts instead of ten eight-hour shifts. This way they have every other Friday off. It didn't necessarily make a difference in the surgery residents' hours, but nevertheless it was a reason to go out and relax.

We had gone to some of these before we got pregnant, but they now became a staple in Conner's schedule. Smoking bans had yet to be passed, so I would not go to bars or the casinos due to the pregnancy. I wasn't eating feta cheese and raw tuna, I certainly wasn't going to breathe smoke-filled air and send that to my baby! Conner slowly became more physically distant from me and the baby during his free time and more interested in his social calendar. Which Elvis impersonator show he was planning to see, or what classic car he would purchase next on eBay was preferable to reading the pregnancy books and keeping a journal with me as we had planned to do weekly.

One night in particular I was excited about the baby kicks I was feeling and reached to put his hand on my abdomen. He pulled it back and said annoyed, "I felt that already."

I was so deeply hurt that night, thinking, *But you haven't felt this kick! And she's changing every day.* We talked about it a few days later, and he didn't seem to think it was insensitive or uncaring.

Around the same time, I had a dream I will never forget. I typically do not remember my dreams. By the time I hit the pillow, my body is so thankful that I get to rest, that my brain shuts off all communication with my conscious mind and memory. But as I had been woken out of a sound sleep when I felt conception, I awoke in a sweat after the murder.

My friend Jackie and I were walking in Manhattan. She had been trying to get pregnant for months. In my dream, we were both pregnant and strolling and shopping as we often had when we lived in the city working on our graduate degrees. We were nicely dressed and feeling beautiful, big, and pregnant. We had walked into a little shop to get some lunch, with shopping bags on our arms. It was a tiny place, standing room only, a counter, and they only served soup. Perfect, a good healthy lunch for us and the growing babies!

Several men worked behind the counter, one at the register, two serving, and others washing dishes in the back. One handed Jackie her cup of soup and bread, and another was handing me mine when a man came rushing toward us from the back of the shop. He grabbed me by the neck, pushing Jackie out of the way and to the ground. He pushed me up against the wall and was pulling up my skirt. My soup fell to the floor, splashing and burning my legs. This man was going to rape me. He was going to hurt my baby. I grabbed a soup ladle that was hanging on the wall behind me. With both hands, I began beating him about the head and neck with the handle of the ladle. He began to stutter-step and fall away from me. I didn't stop. I kept beating him about the head. He started bleeding from his ears and neck. He fell out of the shop and onto the sidewalk. I continued beating him with the heavy ladle. I stood above him and watched the blood pour from his head, neck, and ears. His face was unrecognizable. He was motionless. I turned to make sure Jackie was okay. She was breathless with relief and shock. I stood and waited for the police to come while I held the ladle with my arms crossed.

The sweat drenched my T-shirt, and I woke with my heart racing. I felt engorged with adrenaline. I was empowered and relieved. I had saved my child. I was eating organic foods, taking vitamins, exercising, reading to my belly. My body was a temple for new growth. No man would attempt to hurt my baby. It was the first, and thankfully last, time I have ever dreamt of killing someone. But in those wee hours, I felt more maternal and mammalian than I ever had. I was the mama and I would defend my young. It was instinct.

12
NEW YORK CITY

We decided to travel with another couple, friends of ours who were also pregnant and due about the same time. They too had just found out they were to have a girl. Olivia and I called each other after every check-up to see how the other was doing and what kinds of things we were buying in preparation. Conner had an April conference in New York City, and they would accompany us for some of the time. I had lived in the West Village while getting my master's degree. Mark and Olivia had never been to the city. I looked forward to showing them around and enjoying a little getaway before our babies were born. Olivia and I had been sharing and enjoying our pregnancies together, and this would be a fun trip for us all: plays, dinners out, Central Park, Macy's, Empire State Building. We would do all the touristy things and take lots of pictures of our pregnant bellies!

One night we met up with some college friends of mine. Of course, I wasn't drinking; Pellegrino with lime had become my drink of choice. Conner, on the other hand, started drinking at the first bar.

Whenever someone else was buying, he always seemed to indulge a bit too much. He used to tell stories of how his father would take them to Wendy's or some such place and order baked potatoes for everyone. Potatoes were cheap, and then the three sons could have access to the salad bar without being questioned and stock up. This would be their main meal for the day. Stories like these from his childhood were common. The same thing would happen if my parents were treating us to dinner. Conner would order the 'market-priced' seafood appetizer or the extra topping for his already expensive filet. If someone else was paying the freight, Conner definitely took advantage. I saw this continue even after we were living rather comfortably.

We began the evening at the first bar with a college friend and then we all met up with Mark and Olivia at their hotel lobby bar. They had complimentary drinks provided to them because they had gotten locked *inside* their hotel room for a brief but scary chunk of time earlier that day. Great, more free drinks. Olivia and I were, of course, sober. Thankfully Manhattan had gone smoke free, and all bars and restaurants were a pleasure now. Conner had more drinks.

During this, our second stop for the evening, I pleaded, "Conner, can you please slow down a bit? We've got a really nice dinner ahead."

I had made reservations for the four of us at Le Cirque, a top tier New York City restaurant I knew Mark and Olivia would certainly enjoy. The cab dropped us off, and Olivia and I lingered outside admiring the surrounding architecture and chatting. We entered only a few minutes after the men, but Conner already had a beer in hand. I decided right then I would enjoy my dinner. Conner was his own man. I had done this on many occasions prior. I didn't want to be a mother to two children. He needed to take care of himself and regulate his own drinking.

We had a wonderful round of appetizers and were enjoying the main course when Conner got up to go to the bathroom. Olivia, Mark, and I continued talking.

I hadn't even noticed how much time had passed when Mark said, "Has Conner been gone a while?"

I thought and said, "Yeah, I guess he has."

Mark offered to go check on him. Mark returned a while later and said Conner was throwing up in the bathroom but said he planned to return shortly. I'm sure Le Cirque and its other guests loved the bathroom ambiance my husband was providing. In the meantime, the rest of us had finished our entrees and would be asking for dessert, especially since the couple next to us had a delectable assortment of sweets delivered.

Conner eventually returned to the table, looking white as a sheet, sweaty and clammy.

"I think my lamb was rotten," he said.

I looked sharply into his glassy eyes and said, "Rotten food at a five-star restaurant? I wish I'd had half of what you drank tonight."

I couldn't believe he was trying to lie his way out when we all knew he had been drinking way more than his body could handle.

I looked down and continued to peruse my dessert menu. After about a minute of squirming and presumably trying to focus on the menu he said he would have to excuse himself and would meet us outside. Mark and Olivia were most accommodating, suggesting we not have dessert, but I insisted, saying I was not going to let his drinking ruin a perfectly wonderful dinner. We ate dessert and took some pictures of the two of them before we left.

I walked outside. It was raining. No sign of Conner.

Where could he be? Was he around a corner throwing up on the sidewalk? Where was he? I was alarmed and upset. He was not answering multiple calls to his phone. Who knows where he ended up? Mark, Olivia, and I got a cab, and they dropped me back at my hotel before heading for their own. I apologized profusely for my husband's embarrassing behavior of the evening. They said they understood.

"He has a stressful job. It's not a problem," they said.

But I knew Olivia would have felt the same, or worse, had it been Mark.

I went up to the room after stopping in the lobby to see if Conner might possibly be waiting. I was really beginning to worry. Conner had a poor sense of direction and didn't know the city like I did. He was not in the room. Not two minutes passed and I heard a faint knock. It was him.

His new and best suit covered in rain and muddy, oily water. He must have fallen on the street or sidewalk. His eyes were glassy, his skin and hair soaked, and he still looked clammy. He was a mess, and I was totally frightened by his behavior.

I had seen Conner drink too much before on several occasions, especially during visits with his family. It didn't help that his twin brother could hold three times the beer Conner's system could process. But this was unusual. And not only unusual, but cruel given that we were traveling with close friends, close friends who were also pregnant. This trip was about celebrating our new families to be, and this particular night was the one I looked forward to the most. It would be a pricey dinner, but one surely savored. Wasn't he embarrassed? Why did he do this to me? To our friends? To himself?

Conner didn't know when to stop. After three beers, he would get a little weird. He hadn't been terribly drunk and sick since the night with Nora and Alessandro the year we married, that I knew about. His drinking definitely increased after the pregnancy, and he was going out more without me. He would return home, and I would be long asleep.

And when he drank he would generally get aggressive. He never hit me, but would seem sometimes on the brink of that, getting frustrated easily, sometimes stomping out of the room to be alone, or ending a conversation oddly or abruptly.

And sexually he was always more aggressive in an unattractive way, sometimes grabbing me by the waist, kissing me hard, suggesting we get to bed even if we were out with friends. He always came off desperate and insecure – two qualities I find completely unattractive.

I opened the door and let him in, but said nothing. What was there to say? And it only looked like he would get sick again. We slept in separate beds that night since I didn't want to lay next to him for several reasons, most critically because he was disgustingly dirty with city street grime, vomit, and who knows what else he encountered on his way to the hotel. How did he get back to the hotel?

Another evening in NYC cut short by his drinking. Another evening I would ask all these questions to no one but myself.

The next morning, Conner, was all apologies.

He even admitted for the first time, "I think I have a problem," and promised, "I won't drink for a year."

We had talked about drinking before we got pregnant. I enjoyed a beer or wine with dinners but I wouldn't drink for 9 months, plus the months I planned to nurse. I even stopped drinking once we started trying to get pregnant. He kind of rode the fence during our discussions, but seemed like he thought it was a good idea if he didn't drink while I was pregnant, to show his support. And maybe that's when the heavy closet drinking began.

We had planned to meet Mark and Olivia for breakfast the next morning. Conner threw up into a large planter on the street on our walk toward their hotel. I bought him water and ginger ale from a vendor and helped wipe his mouth with a napkin. He kept apologizing and seemed truly mortified. There he was, in broad daylight vomiting in public into a beautiful flower planter in midtown Manhattan. I was embarrassed enough for both of us. But I decided I had better look away and get my bagel and cream cheese down before I started feeling morning sickness.

We greeted Mark and Olivia, and Conner immediately apologized and begged forgiveness for his behavior the night before. He told them he wouldn't drink for a year as his penance, he called it. I was happy because I thought that meant he wouldn't be drinking for the rest of the pregnancy and then even after the baby was born.

13
GENOA

I was riding in the car with my dad home from dinner. As we drove over the bridge something must have seemed unusual to him.

"Julie, are you okay?" he asked.

"Yeah, I'm fine."

I guess I was unusually quiet. I was tired and anxious to meet my baby girl. An hour or so later at the house I began painful contractions that brought me to the floor.

Conner and I had not been to any birthing classes. He had delivered a dozen babies in med school. With his work schedule, we wouldn't have been able to attend a regular class anyway. I didn't want to attend a birth class without my husband. I would feel the need to explain why he wasn't there. I decided reading and watching videos would be enough. I read and learned every day on my own in my professional work. And women do this every day, don't they? I could handle it.

Two weeks before my due date I was dilated four centimeters. My parents decided to change their flights since the doctor said I could go at any time. They wanted to welcome Genoa into the world too. After they arrived we waited and waited. They had come early, and now Genoa decided to take her time.

Mom and I went and had a pedicure. I put little smiley face stickers on my big toes so I would have a pick me up when in labor. My hospital bag was packed with cameras and clothes. At the house, diapers were ready, and all of her teeny, tiny soft clothes sat washed and waiting. We would practice attachment parenting, breast feeding, co-sleeping, and baby wearing. Her little co-sleeper was attached to our king bed ready to welcome her to our family.

We got to the hospital late the night of August 12. The contractions were jolting and grew more intense. I knew I didn't have too far to go before an epidural since I was already walking around quite dilated. It was like no other pain I've ever experienced. The nurses on the floor were terribly condescending, reminding us all it was my first pregnancy and the pain probably wasn't that bad yet. But I kept thinking, *I was dilated 4 centimeters last week, ladies!* They didn't want to call the doctor yet because it was too soon. Meanwhile, no one had checked my cervix.

Finally, I was torquing and twisting in the bed so much with pain that my parents stepped out of the room.

I grabbed Conner by the shirt and said, "Get me a fucking doctor!"

"I'm a doctor," he stuttered.

As if suddenly enlightened, he put his gloves on to measure my cervix and sure enough she was making her way down. The doctor arrived shortly thereafter, ordered the epidural, and got me to the delivery room. Once I received the epidural, the pain subsided, but everything slowed down. We moved all our belongings into the new room, along with a 3D ultrasound photo of Genoa. I wanted to be able to see her little face while I was pushing.

I was pushing, but not effectively. This went on for hours. I later found out there were issues with my tailbone.

Five other women were also in active labor that night. A 'busy day' at this facility was delivering TWO babies, and they had all FIVE of us on the brink of delivery. It must have been the full moon and the luck of Friday the 13th. They were simply overwhelmed running between patients. The doctors and nurses were nowhere to be seen.

My parents, Conner, and I were left with one labor and delivery technician. However, at one point she said, "I'm sorry but I'm feeling a bit sick. I'm pregnant and need to go sit down."

We couldn't believe it; the one shred of help we had was now about to pass out.

Conner, Mom, and Dad had all seen the heart rate drop now for the second time. The monitor was behind my head so I was not aware of the severity of the situation, but could tell from their eyes things were getting tense. I was content not to be writhing in pain anymore.

Conner took the reins, and as my mother recalled, "He was like steel."

He looked at my parents and said, "This is a family event, and we need to get this baby out. I'm going to need your help. Can each of you come on this side of the bed and hold a leg."

I was not really thrilled with the thought of my mother or my father seeing me in quite that position and from quite that angle.

I said, "No, let's just try again first."

Well, she still wasn't coming down anymore, so Dad held one leg and my mom the other. We were a close knit family, but none of us expected to be quite this close or involved in Genoa's birth. Conner could now feel Genoa's little head, and I was doing my best to push with my parents serving as clamps for my legs. She started to crown.

The OB came in and not a minute soon! She was calm and relaxed. She asked Conner if he wanted to deliver the baby. He asked her to set up an extension to the table to eliminate the chance of Genoa falling to the floor. Conner and the OB delivered Genoa with Mom and Dad close at hand.

It was an amazing emotional relief in so many ways. Her color was good and her Apgar score high. They cleaned her up quickly. Conner and I had requested we get to bond with her for an hour before they did any tests or put antibiotic in her eyes that would blur her vision. I had read that the trauma of the birth was so significant that providing babies the immediate opportunity to bond, smell, and see us would be critical. Her face and eyes were a bit swollen, but otherwise she was completely alert and intrigued by her new surroundings.

Later she easily latched on and was nursing. It was truly an unparalleled moment for me: my child at my breast, my husband at my side, and my parents there to witness their growing family.

We returned from the hospital the next day, even though they wanted us to stay another day. Genoa had a bowel movement, and I was feeling great. Besides, Conner didn't want to spend any more time in his work place than absolutely necessary. We wanted to bring our baby home.

What an exceptional sensation it was to bring a newborn home, to welcome her to her new life and surround her with love and comfort. We documented the momentous arrival on the front steps with pictures and video, unlocked the front door, and Genoa was home.

We sat in the living room relieved Genoa was healthy and safe after the last exhausting 36 hours. We played and listened tearfully to the song 'Genoa' sung by Andre Deluca. Our daughter was named after the northern Italian city on the sea, not because she was conceived there as many a nosey friend has asked, but because I wanted a location name. My grandmother was named Florence, I have a great Aunt Virginia and like the strength and permanence that comes with a location name. In addition, Genoa seemed perfect because of Deluca's beautiful song about love in that city. This little girl would be surrounded by love, her life full of travel and exploration, and hopefully she too would develop a love of music. Rose, her middle name, would be reminder of where our love began on Roseman Bridge. She was an extension of that love and those promises.

"Genoa, an impressive name indeed," a man once said in passing in the New York City library near Bryant Park. He looked kindly into her three year old blue eyes and said almost in a whisper, "Something I can tell you will live up to, my dear."

14
UNFORGETTABLE

My parents and sisters had just left to travel back to Connecticut. My parents had been in the delivery room, and my sisters came down shortly afterwards to cuddle and pamper their new niece. Now that I was sort of settled in with the new baby, this would be our first holiday weekend as a new family of three.

Conner had the Labor Day weekend off and decided he would like to take a little family trip. Genoa was less than a month old. I was tired; I found nursing much more draining than being pregnant. And little Genoa was an eater. I dropped my pregnancy weight rapidly, and had to work to stay hydrated and healthy. Conner always wanted to be running and doing and have 'plans.' So for the holiday weekend he decided he wanted to get away. I was not really keen on the idea of traveling with a 3 week old, but she was healthy and portable, so I went along with his idea. I tried not to think too much about the germs she would encounter in a hotel room. "I'm building her immune system," became my mantra.

We decided to leave Saturday afternoon and drive to Tuscaloosa, stroll around the University of Alabama campus, and enjoy the little college town together. I love university towns, coffee shops, and book stores. This would be a relaxing way to spend the holiday weekend together as a new family of three. But before we left, his college was playing Notre Dame.

"It will be a blow out," he said.

But Conner wanted to go and watch a 'little bit' of the game, probably not even to halftime, at a casino.

"Sure, I know this is your weekend off. Go out enjoy the game. I'll get us all packed up for the trip."

I knew football games were part of Conner's past, and it seemed like he needed a little down time.

"Okay, thanks. I'll watch only a little bit of the game. It'll be too hard to watch more than that anyway," he said.

"And then we'll head out sometime early afternoon-ish?"

"Sounds about right, I'll be back in a bit." He kissed me goodbye.

He left around 11am. I worked in between breastfeeding and diaper changes to pack wipes, diapers, pajamas, burp cloths, baby soap, soft washcloths, blankets, books, activity mat, vitamins, clothes for myself that fitted my post-birth body which was quickly returning to normal, camera, video camera, snacks for the drive, lots of drinks to keep me hydrated and full of milk, stroller, Baby Bjorn and baby sling.

Around 12:30, I called Conner's cell phone to ask him which car he wanted to take so I could start packing the car, but he didn't answer. If he were in a casino, sometimes the reception could be spotty. I waited.

It was now close to 1pm. The first half would surely have been over by now. I went online to check the score. Notre Dame was well ahead. I tried to call again, still no answer. I tried to page him, no answer. I started to worry. He said he would only be gone for an hour or two, would only watch the first half at most, and if it was a blow-out even less. I busied myself with packing, nursing, and keeping Genoa happy. I hoped she would sleep in the car so we could have some couple time and planned to keep her awake until we left.

Another 30 minutes, still no word from Conner. It was 1:30. I called the sports bar at the Bluewater Casino. The Bluewater was just minutes from our home. I remembered what he was wearing even with my post-pregnancy brain. It was an unusual Hawaiian style shirt, with green and cream panels with four small palm trees on it. His father had given him the shirt last Christmas.

The bartender at the Bluewater sports bar didn't have the game on any of his TVs. Okay, where could he be? I tried a few other casinos. Most of them had few, if anyone, sitting watching the games, so it was easy for them to tell me if Conner was there.

I decided to call Hooters. We had always kind of teased about Hooters and what a trashy place it was. I had never been in a Hooters restaurant and didn't plan on supporting the establishment.

"Yes," she said over the phone, "He was here. Green shirt with palm trees, real friendly guy. He just left." I thanked the nice bartender and waited for Conner to call.

The call finally came about 15 minutes later. The game had been completely over now for at least 30 minutes.

"Hey, I'm on my way home," he said.

"It was a blow-out?" I asked.

"Yeah."

"So where did you go?"

"I was at the Bluewater. I'll be home in twenty minutes."

The Bluewater is only about five minutes from the house. I decided to confront him.

"I know you weren't at the Bluewater, Conner. Think about it on your drive and then you can tell me the truth when you get here."

"What? ... I'll see you in a bit." He acted like he didn't know what I was talking about.

"Okay." And I ended the call.

Genoa was consumed by sleep. I couldn't keep her awake anymore. I laid her down in her room. I was happy to have a few minutes of quiet before Conner got home to collect my thoughts. I sat in our sunroom looking across the lush green lawn that I had mowed the week before. My neighbors thought I was crazy and that I needed to heal more. But it felt good to do physical labor and be outside sweating. I loved the place called Bridal Lane. And I especially loved the fall. It was time for school, new students that semester, a new routine, a new baby, a new life.

Conner pulled up in front of the house in our half circle drive. I greeted him as he came in the front door and asked him to sit with me in the sunroom. We sat across from each other, round glass table between us. My hands were folded in my lap.

"Where did you go to watch the game?" I began.

"I told you already. I was at the Bluewater." He lied straight into my eyes. I couldn't believe he was so good at this.

"Oh, really," I said calmly. "Are you sure? I'll give you another chance to tell me the truth."

"I was at the Bluewater. I just decided to watch the whole game. And then I lost track of time. You know phones don't have service there."

"I know where you were. I'll give you one last chance, or would you prefer I tell you where you were?"

He stared at me blankly.

"The bartender at Hooters said you were 'real friendly.' Were you drinking?"

"I just had a couple. I knew I'd be driving later."

Genoa started whimpering a bit in the bedroom and needed comforting. I spent several minutes with her, and she fell back to sleep. When I returned to the sunroom, Conner's shirt was hanging on the back of the chair and I was confused.

"Conner? Conner? Where are you?"

I walked through the long sunroom, through the guest room, and into the guest bath. He was vomiting at the toilet.

"Oh, my God, Conner, are you okay?"

I ran and got washcloths, some ice to put on his head and neck. He was violently ill. I'd never seen anything like it. I thought maybe it was food poisoning. This couldn't be the result of a couple of beers.

Genoa started crying again, and I ran back across the house to her. She needed to be fed and would eat for twenty minutes on each side. I cradled her, nursing. She was still so young, but I didn't want her to see him or be scared by the noises she was hearing. But I couldn't wait half an hour to check on him. I returned to the bathroom.

He was still kneeling in front of the toilet, his back and torso convulsing as he continued nonstop vomiting and dry heaving. The smell was horrible. I flushed the toilet for him and wiped his face while mindful not to hit Genoa's head on the toilet or bathroom wall. When she finished nursing on one side, she seemed peaceful and ready to go back to sleep. I returned her to her co-sleeper.

I got some more ice and a cold glass of water and returned to the bathroom. Conner was now lying on his back on the floor of the shower. The shower water was running on him, and the smell almost made me vomit. He was still clothed wearing his undershirt, pants, belt, and shoes. What was he doing? Then I realized what had happened. Conner had urinated and defecated in his pants. He had vomit and saliva drooling from his mouth. He had crawled from the toilet to the shower and now laid in his own shit. What the hell was happening to my husband?

I cried in fear and kept asking what I could do. I had never seen Conner like this and had no idea how I was going to be able to help or move this 6'2", 175lb man. He told me he wanted to lay there. When I flushed the toilet I realized the vomit smelled of beer. Could this be alcohol induced? Even in my college days I had not seen someone this sick.

I knelt by the shower door, unbuckled his pants a bit for comfort, and took his shoes off. I wiped his face and turned the water cooler when he asked. He lay motionless, pale.

I couldn't believe what I was looking at. I squatted in my carpeted bathroom. I ran my fingers through my hair and held my head in my hands. Was this the father of my beautiful child? Was this the man who promised not to drink for a year in New York City four months ago? Was this man an officer in the U.S. military and a surgeon responsible for the lives of people in their greatest time of need? Conner graduated top of his class. Was I really looking at the best our military had to offer?

I was overcome with disgust and hate. I wanted him to disappear. I wanted to spit on him. I got my camera. He needed to see what he had become from the outside. He needed to know what he was doing to himself. He needed never to forget this day because I would never forget this day. I took a picture of him lying on the shower floor, fully clothed, pants unzipped, water spraying and running over him, no color in his skin, drool oozing from his mouth. His face appeared dead. The flash went off and startled him. He reached his left hand to cover his groin. I took another picture. He asked me to stop. I did.

Hours later, still in the shower, I finally asked him quietly and gently, "Did you really just have a couple drinks, Conner?"

"Yes, it was just two."

"How could that be? I even saw blood in the toilet, Conner. I would be taking you to the hospital, if you didn't work there."

I wanted to save Conner the embarrassment of an ER visit since he would be sure to be treated by physicians he knew, and I would have to explain what happened. Besides, I had a newborn whom I did not want to expose to hospital germs. Building her immune system was one thing, but exposing her to the emergency room at 3 weeks old, seemed irresponsible and dangerous.

Hours passed. Conner still lay in the shower. *I guess we're not going to Tuscaloosa for the weekend.* Genoa woke from her afternoon nap. I changed her diaper, breastfed, and kept checking on my husband on the shower floor. He was not able to hold down even sips of water without vomiting it back up. Early evening he started gagging blood again. It was not huge amounts, but blood splattered his shirt and shower floor. I kept thinking I should take him to the hospital, but he kept telling me he would be fine.

"I just need to lie here a bit longer."

Late that night he finally told me. He did drink two beers, but one of them was a pitcher and the other was a pint. He drank an entire pitcher and a pint of beer. This was a man who could barely handle three 12 oz cans. And then he drove 20 minutes home! And who knows if that was the truth. Thank God no one else was hurt. Thank God Genoa wasn't with him. Thank God, Genoa and I didn't get in a packed car with him to drive to Tuscaloosa.

My mind had lots of wander time that Labor Day weekend. Had he done this before? He seemed amazingly skilled and confident while lying to me earlier, both on the phone and face-to-face. This was a man who used to stutter and get red in the face with embarrassment when he told a little white lie. Maybe I couldn't read him anymore. Maybe other drinking events occurred that I hadn't noticed. Maybe there were other *things* going on I hadn't noticed. My mind raced but not in hurried fashion, rather it was slowly reviewing and remembering times since I got pregnant almost a year ago.

Something quite simply died inside me that day. I became afraid I might never love him the way I did before. It felt as though I was preparing to vomit as I walked around looking at life. I was weary unpacking all the baby clothes and toys. I watched my hands as they worked, detached from my worried mind. There, sparkling among the baby clothes I saw my engagement ring, my deeply-flawed diamond. A flaw you could only see if you looked at it just so. A large expensive-looking stone, but cracked at its core. My heart was numb, my trust dead.

In a marriage or any relationship, we experience disappointment from time to time. People let us down, and we learn to love and accept them and vice versa. Conner and I had some rough spots. We'd been together nine years. Of course, we had difficult times, especially when dealing with his family. But nothing was irreparable, nothing that I couldn't accept and work around or accommodate. Marriage, my word, and my promises were forever.

That night I felt different. In the past, his drinking only impacted and embarrassed me. Today, this disappointment, this failure impacted our new family, our baby. A brand new little family that as of yesterday was sweet and pure. I was hurting for myself and my child. What would her future be like? Conner's parents were alcoholics. Would Genoa grow up with an alcoholic father? Was Conner scared of being a parent? What was wrong with him? What was he hiding or trying to bury with alcohol?

Conner had made comments months before that he was worried about being a good role model and not knowing how to treat a little girl. He said he was looking forward to the days when she was older, and they could work on his cars together. But the baby years, those would be mine.

I'd laughed, rolled my eyes and said, "You can't suddenly decide you're going to bond with a child when they're six! It starts now. Actually it started months ago, and all through the pregnancy when she was beginning to hear and recognize our voices. That's why I was reading books to my tummy every day."

Conner was an overly proud man, so for him to express any kind of fear should have been a warning to me.

I never felt the same for Conner after Labor Day for a combination of emotions and causes. Our first weekend together as a new family ruined, his heavy irresponsible daytime drinking - and driving, the ironic choice of Hooters while I sat home breastfeeding our child, burping my infant child and wiping her spit up, only then to wipe his face of vomit and shower feces from his body. What hurt more?

Something was dead. I grieved for my perfect, healthy little child. Maybe her life wouldn't be so perfect. I never dreamed I would have to shield my daughter's face so she wouldn't see her drunken father lying in his own feces.

I was sad that day not only for my daughter, but also for a friend I lost a dozen years earlier around Labor Day. He was driving a Jeep that ran off the road and into a tree. I had been a passenger. Seth was killed instantly. While speculations flew that drinking had been involved, an autopsy would later prove he was sober, and the cause of the accident remains unknown to this day.

It was a tragic start to that academic year; death, mortality, love, and loss. I spent 10 days in the hospital and had two surgeries that fall. I completed the semester and was accepted into graduate programs that December. My life continued as planned, but Seth's dreams, those of his parents, and the lives around him were irreparably wounded. I always think of Seth and his family on Labor Day.

As I cradled Genoa that afternoon, I thought how I would work endlessly to protect her. I'm sure Seth's parents had those same feelings and dreams for their only son. How cruel and unexpected life can be for parents. I've heard it said being a parent is like letting your heart walk around outside your body for the rest of your life.

Conner was finally able to get to his feet after almost seven hours in the shower. He eventually took a real shower. I washed his clothes out, and he went to bed.

The next morning began with more promises. This time he was positive he had a drinking problem and decided again, without my prompting, that he should stop drinking altogether, forever.

I was surprised at this declaration. Especially when it was coupled with, "I know there's alcoholism in my family. It's genetic. And I need to be careful not to fall into its trap."

This promise lasted no longer than two weeks following several conversations with Jonathan, his twin. Jonathan thought Conner was being too drastic and he should instead pace his drinking. Maybe it would be a good idea for Conner to drink a couple beers every night to build up his tolerance.

"Tolerance?" I asked. "Tolerance for what? Are you joining a fraternity?"

It was ridiculous. I couldn't keep talking about his drinking. Jonathan had such an emotional hold on Conner, it was hard to ever change Conner's mind once Jonathan had planted an idea. It was too painful and I felt it a waste of my energy. Stopping all together seemed drastic but what he had done and his drinking habits over the past year probably warranted something drastic.

I couldn't control how he drank. I learned that long ago. I had a baby to breastfeed, a tub and faucets to pick out for the master suite addition under construction, two undergraduate courses that were starting late due to Genoa's birth, and a half million dollar grant to oversee. I had a life that had to go on whether Conner was drunk or not.

So our version of family life went on. Conner lived away nine of the next twelve months with surgery training rotations all across the region. I was essentially a single working parent at home. I don't know what his daily drinking patterns were during that time. If I asked, I was badgering him, so I simply chose not to ask. It didn't seem to be helping either of us.

I wasn't drinking at all because I breastfed for nine months. We went to visit Conner or he came home just about every other weekend or more often. When we saw him he always had a few beers with dinner, but nothing that bordered on drunkenness. I would sometimes find empty beer cans in the bushes when I mowed the lawn, nothing more.

But the raw memories of Labor Day and my fears could not be alleviated. I avoided them with more pressing issues around work, research, and teaching, raising a child, keeping up with her baby book, photos, and videos, and keeping a house up and running, bills, lawn, trash, and laundry, with my husband living away.

At the time, I thought I suffered from postpartum depression. I probably suffered from general depression and feelings of abandonment. But I *wanted* us to continue working toward our dreams. Our daughter Genoa was now part of that dream and I feared we both were slowly and deliberately being pushed out of Conner's life.

The months he lived at home, he spent more and more time working in the garage on his cars. He would come home from a busy day and instead of wanting to spend time with me or Genoa, he would grab a beer, turn up Elvis or Johnny Cash, and sometimes not come in from the garage until bedtime. Some nights I was hoping for a little relief as I had been a caregiver all day. Other nights I needed to get some work done. I had deadlines for conferences and journal articles, and needed him to take over. But I quickly learned not to expect much.

He would call and say he was going out with the single guys after work to casinos or the bar for 'just a couple of drinks.' I never knew what was going to walk through the door those nights. Other nights I would stay up late after Genoa was asleep working, doing dishes, laundry, and Conner would come up from the garage and be dead asleep minutes later, before I could make it up to bed.

Genoa was still so young and most nights required a feeding or a diaper change in the wee hours. I was almost always the one to get up, even though he was only home for a few weeks at a time and even then some of those nights were spent at the hospital. More often than not, Conner wouldn't even hear Genoa's cries during the night and trying to wake him was often more difficult than just going to her myself. I even remember two nights in particular when I came up to bed after working in my home office. I touched him gently, his back, stomach, hips, and stroked him to wake him up. He was out cold. No waking him. I even rolled him over but there was no sign of consciousness.

15
HAPPY BIRTHDAY, BABY!

August 2005

My family all wanted to spend Genoa's first birthday together. Conner was in Miami Beach for three months doing trauma training. He was unable to leave Miami, so the party would have to go to him. My parents and sisters arranged for time away from work and flights that would put them all in Miami Beach for her birthday. We would celebrate Genoa's new little life for the weekend.

Genoa and I flew into Miami several days ahead to have some time with Conner and make plans for the birthday party. The whole family arrived a few days later. They would be spending their time at a hotel on the strip because Conner's military condominium, although spacious, would not be comfortable for six people and a toddling baby. Four flights and four nights in a hotel in Miami Beach was an expensive trip. But it was worth it to mark Genoa's 365th day on the planet together. She was 12 months old and thriving.

Before I arrived, Conner had purchased over $350 of trinkets at a local party store for the birthday party we planned to have at his condo. We laughed that it was difficult to spend that much money at a party store. He bought balloons and helium tank; multiple rolls of streamers; a string of paper lanterns; a huge six foot inflatable parrot; matching plates and napkins; elaborate party hats for each of us; including a pirate, a queen, a juggler; a first year bib and assortment of first year candles for Genoa; a bubble machine; and large party horns. Looking back, it was quite the show. Would one-year old Genoa appreciate all of this? Or was this more an opportunity for Conner to show how much he loved Genoa? Nine days later he would email me for a divorce. Why all the pomp and circumstance? Because it would be our last event as a family?

I arranged for takeout trays of seafood and pasta from a local Italian restaurant and a beautiful fruit-topped cake – with "Happy Birthday Genoa" from a local Brazilian bakery. It would be an international event in a mostly Spanish speaking city for our daughter named Genoa. I was excited to have everyone together for a fun birthday weekend.

During the day, we went to the Miami Aquarium. It was a hot day with little overhead cloud coverage. Conner was jumpy and worried about everyone's comfort levels.

"Julie, we need to do something, everyone's really hot. They're really uncomfortable. Do something."

"It's August - in Florida." I replied. "Not much we can do, Conner. Just relax. Go buy a water. Cool off."

Genoa enjoyed walking around, seeing the birds and the manatees. The whole morning Conner was rushing us through everything so we wouldn't be uncomfortable, but he just succeeded in making everyone even more uncomfortable because he was so tense. We got to the dolphin show finally. We sat down, and it was an ordeal deciding how we would sit along the bench. Conner couldn't decide where to sit. He wanted to be next to Genoa, but Genoa wanted to sit with her aunts. I drizzled cold water on her head to distract her, hoping the situation would be resolved. Conner sat in front of my sisters so he could hold Genoa on his lap, and she could still make faces at her aunts behind her. Every decision, movement, and arrangement was an ordeal. My nerves throbbed until we got back in the car.

Back at the condo we split up. Grandma and Grandpa spent the late afternoon with Genoa at the pool while Conner and I prepared the condo for the party. Conner and I ran around picking up the food, cake, and getting everything ready. Conner wanted Genoa to be surprised when she came into the 'party' at his condo with the helium balloons, inflated parrot, lights, and show. He was nervous and edgy. He was so concerned about everything going right – the food, the decorations, et cetera. I put my hands on his shoulders as we stood in the kitchen.

Looking into his eyes, I said, "This is a party for a one-year-old. She won't remember this at all," motioning to the table of trinkets. "This is really a little party for the adults to enjoy Genoa enjoying herself. And it's just my family. Why are you so stressed out today?"

"I'm not stressed. I just want everything to be perfect for our little honey." His anxiety was unwarranted. But maybe he was dealing with many more issues than I knew. It was almost as if this was a manic episode of sorts. He was wired.

The food was delicious and the evening fun overall, but I had to talk to him during the party again, taking him aside in the tiny kitchen.

"Conner, slow down! You are jumping up and down. It's stressing everyone out. The food is hot, the cake is cool, it's all gonna be okay."

He left the kitchen abruptly, and went into the bedroom. He returned with the tiny rocking horse he had painted red, blue, and yellow for Genoa. We had picked it out months ago, and he had just finished it.

"I'm going to give this to her now."

"But people are still eating." He looked at me disappointed. "Fine, go ahead. She'll love it!"

At the end of the party after Genoa had enjoyed lots of spaghetti and shrimp as evidenced by the sauce all over her face followed by her fruit topped cake, Conner volunteered to put Genoa to bed. This was rare for him to do. He disappeared into the bedroom, and they fell asleep. The rest of us cleaned up. I was relieved he was out for the night and would be working the whole next 24 hours.

Maybe Conner knew then this would be his last birthday as Genoa's 'Daddy,' since later he would ask her to call him 'Daddy

Conner' predicting there might someday be another father figure in her life that she would call 'Daddy.' Maybe Conner was thinking more about creating his own memory of his young child's face in awe of all the colored balloons and hats. The whole birthday weekend remains a mystery to me.

Christine would soon attend nursing school and Conner had arranged for her to shadow him at the hospital on Sunday. I spent the day with my parents and Genoa at the Parrot Jungle enjoying all the gorgeous birds. Elizabeth stayed behind to do some work.

After Hurricane Katrina, Christine shared with me the events of that day. The most telling thing she said was, "Conner is a totally different person at work." She was surprised at how 'cool' he was compared to the front he had for me and the family.

On their less than ten minute drive to the hospital she said, "He dropped the f-bomb at least five times. I was shocked."

All day he was a different version of the Conner she had always known; in the manner he was telling jokes, making small talk, et cetera. I had accompanied Conner to the hospital one afternoon during medical school. This was long before his decision to become a surgeon or his significantly increased responsibilities as a resident. I began to think, how many different Conners were there?

My family all flew back home the next day. Genoa and I stayed on one more day before we flew back to Mississippi.

Nine days later Conner's email would read:

> *We both could probably be happier apart ...*
> *I need a change no matter the cost*

16
BRIDAL LANE

Monday 29 August 2005

Jim pulled up as far as we could on Bridal Lane. The road was completely covered with fallen trees and debris. We couldn't even walk down the street, never mind drive a vehicle. Genoa was asleep in the car lying across the back seat with her head on my lap. Jim and Laura set out to venture down the Lane to try to see their home.

Suddenly I received a text message. I'd been trying to get through on the phones all day. Something must have connected. I tried to call my mother again in Connecticut. She and Elizabeth answered, crying with joy to hear my voice and know we were alive. I told them about the devastation we had already seen, the Jackson Bridge gone, the flooding everywhere, homes with complete sides ripped from them with furniture waiting for the owners to return and relax with a sweet tea.

"Jim and Laura just headed down Bridal. Genoa is asleep but when they get back I'll head down too."

Mom said through tears, "Call me when you see your house, Julie. I want to be with you. I don't want you to do this alone."

"Mom," I inhaled. "I need to do this by myself. This was our home. And he's not here. I must go alone."

I thought the end was beginning - and I was ready. Katrina had given me my answer.

"Please don't worry. I'm going to be okay. It's just stuff. Genoa and I are okay. A house doesn't make a home."

She kept saying, "Okay, Julie," while she wept.

"And if it's gone, Mom, which I'm fairly sure it is, I told you we couldn't see the crow's nest from the bridge, it's a sign. I don't need an Mrs. I have a Ph.D. and no one can ever take that from me. I'm going to be okay, Mom. You and Dad gave me an education. That's all I'll ever need in this life … You've given me everything … everything I need."

"Okay," she said exhaling, "I love you so much. I wish I could be there. But I'm so happy you two are with Jim and Laura."

"I'll call you as soon as I know more. But trust that for now *we - are - safe*. Genoa is too young to understand any of this, thank God." I was feeling incredibly strong, prepared, and alive like I did two nights before with my friends. "Mom, I am ready."

"Okay, Julie. We are there with you in spirit." Crying she added, "We love you so much."

I was crying but almost laughing. I knew it was gone. It was just stuff. And all that 'stuff' connected me to him. My life would go on without him. And without our stuff it would be even easier to let go.

I saw Laura climb over a fallen tree coming back toward the car. I wiped my eyes. She said it was too treacherous for her. She couldn't make it through all the debris, the trees, and the power lines. I couldn't sit and wait to hear a report from Jim. I had to try to make it down to 22. Laura said she would stay with sleeping Genoa in the car.

I set out climbing over trees and limbs, through yards trying to avoid power lines. I talked to myself the whole time. My mind was alert. I felt urgency like never before. What was I stepping on? Could there be bodies under all of this? *Keep moving toward your goal.* I climbed over fences.

The sky started to brighten despite the dense foliage and debris overhead. Tears streamed. Visibility was at a minimum. I tried to make my way down the south side of the street. The homes had deep lots, and there might be more room to maneuver. I came to some electrical fencing. I couldn't find the end of it.

I grabbed a stick to test if it might be live. Fortunately it wasn't, and I climbed over, catching my wet wide pant leg and almost falling on my back. I was wearing my favorite Anne Klein summer sandals. I hadn't thought to evacuate with protective footwear.

The houses to my left looked mostly intact. I ran when I could, watching each step carefully. I flashed back to the woods where I grew up in Connecticut. I would race through trails in the woods as a kid on foot hunting for new fern, berries, and jack-in-the-pulpits. My heart was racing again. What might be lingering in these woods? People? Dead or alive? Bodies, body parts? Then I saw a figure about 50 yards away near a home. It was a man; his T-shirt soiled and sweaty. He was staggering. He moved toward the driveway and presumably toward the street. He continued to stagger, and my fight or flight response kicked in. Laura was in the car with the keys, and the doors were locked, right?

I waved quickly and kept running. Soon after I heard voices and saw two figures, a man and a boy. It was Peter, our alderman, and his teenage son. They lived about quarter mile from my house.

"Hey, Peter, it's Julie. We live down at 22. How's the rest of your family? Joyce?"

"Everyone's good, good, thanks. We needed to get out for a bit and see what's left. Where y'all?"

"Husband's outta town with military work in Miami. Baby, dog, and I went with Jim and Laura to their office just south of I-10. It's across from the fire station there."

"How do you think things are going to be down there?" he asked.

"Well, I couldn't see my third floor addition – you know, the crow's nest, from the Paix Bayou Bridge. I'm thinking mine's pretty gone, but who knows? We could see the side wall of Brian's house from the bridge, so that's good. How about you? Any news?"

"No telling. I need to get down there."

"Yeah, me too." I'd already lost time chatting. We all walked a bit together. Peter's son and I climbed over another six-foot fence. When Peter followed he landed hard and twisted his ankle.

He said he was okay, but he was limping and sat to check it. He told me to go ahead. Good. I had to keep moving.

I started running and could now see what looked like pavement and the street in the distance. I made my way to the north and could see the street more clearly now, but there was a six-foot iron fence with no foot holds. I wouldn't be able to climb over this one. I ran back and forth along the fence looking for an opening. I felt like a dog trying to get free, running end to end. I was frantic, trapped, searching for a way out. A way out to the street would lead to my house.

I decided to move some logs and rocks and hurdled the fence landing hard on my sandaled feet. The street was clear and the sky opened. Light shone down on the street! I could see clearly for the first time since we pulled onto Bridal Lane. The foliage was not as heavy here and fewer trees had fallen. I ran down the street. I was panting, my head on a swivel looking from one side to the other.

"Oh, my God ... oh, my God ... oh, my God," was all I could say. I was yelling out at every new sight.

I was running fast, tasting the salty wind, my heart pounding but beating in anticipation, not fear. Some houses were collapsed into themselves; some pulled onto their own front porches. Others had private contents all over their front yards. I hurdled power lines and debris at a full run. I was running so strong and free.

A stretch of 100 yards was completely wide open on the street. My arms and hands swung heavy at my sides, not like my days as a college athlete. My pants' legs were soaked with water, mud, and muck from the knees down. My small frame and boney pelvis barely held them up. My open toed sandals were filled with water, and although my hands and feet were covered with scratches and cuts, I couldn't feel any of them, just the salty air pounding into the back of my throat.

Dead stop in the street.

Melody's house sat in the middle of our street. Her roof was across the entire expanse. It was the Land of Oz. Her house was sucked from its foundation and dropped in the middle of the road. The ditches were filled with water, bikes, curtains, dishes, couches, tables, toys, toys, and more toys. How would her little children live through this? How would Kate and little Mike handle seeing their belongings all over the street? How would Melody and Mike stay strong for their children and still be able to grieve their own loss, anger, and devastation? Thank God Genoa was only one. I was her home and she was mine. Together we would run free.

I needed to get over her roof. Jim must be ahead since I hadn't seen him yet. He must have gone over this roof, and he weighed at least two of me.

I thought, *You're a single mom now, you can't leave Genoa to grow up alone.* If I fell through, Jim would have to come back this way, and I could yell up from below and he would get me out. If I did fall through, what was under there? I have to get to 22. What about Genoa? Okay, try to go a little ways up the roof. Shifting, movement, cracking – all bad.

I tried to go around, to walk through the waist high water. What was in the water? How deep was it? What kind of chemicals, snakes, alligators, bodies? Jim would save me if needed.

I tried again, moving quickly and lightly. I made it across, such a feeling of accomplishment. I leapt off the roof and continued in a dash down the street. It was clear again.

The road widened and made a large bend. A wind gust hit me. I had a hard time staying vertical. I began running crouched closer to the ground. Now that I was on the peninsula with the Gulf on my left and Bayou on the right, the wind was more turbulent. Gulf waters churned waves with large white caps onto the street. The wind blew branches and debris through the air. I shielded my eyes and kept moving. The reward outweighed the risk. I needed to do this. I needed to do this now. I needed to do this alone.

I was alive and so free. I would have no attachments. I would have nothing, no earthly belongings. I would be free of it all. I ran in a race to the finish, but I was running and racing to face my predator, to face my future. I knew what I was going to see at 22.

Without houses, trees, mailboxes, cars, piers, and boathouses as landmarks, I was disoriented. It was a mess of fallen telephone poles, sheets, and clothing in trees. Cars had been whipped and thrown into the middle of formerly manicured lawns. My neighbors' two storey brick looked okay at first, until I looked from the front and could see through the home's first floor to the water beyond. Just beyond, stood Jim and Laura's house. It was standing. The bottom had been washed away, but a lot of structure remained. Wait. What, what was in between? Why was Frannie's car in my front yard? There were my steps ...

I had walked up those steps cuddling my newborn little girl this time last year. She was dressed in a yellow and white handmade outfit my parents bought in Costa Rica. She was a tiny angel. We took pictures of her on those front steps. Happy pictures of a new family of three. I was wearing a cute little dress and looked healthy even though I'd given birth the day before. The Webers, an older couple who lived across the street, walked to see the new baby and helped welcome her home to Bridal Lane.

I remembered saying to my mom shortly after we entered our home, "Now I know what you mean. When you bring a baby back to a home, it makes it a very special place for always."

Conner had picked out this house for me. The view, the bayou, the pelicans, the breezes, sitting on the swing hanging from the live oak, made it all worth the mortgage. We watched the fireworks every Sunday night from that front porch. It was a happy place in the beginning.

I leaned over with my hands on my knees, panting, gasping. I tried to steady myself, both from the wind and the shock. The shock of what I saw, and what I was not seeing. Devastation surrounded me. Clouds raced overhead and strange wisps of cloud whirled at ground level around my shins.

Steps to nowhere ... I walked up the stairs, around the fallen brick pillars and marsh grass. An intact Waterford cake plate sat on the concrete slab. Another dish that had been on the nightstand upstairs, appeared next to a lawnmower. I remembered those moments in front of my dresser. The nightstand was nowhere to be seen.

My lungs filled with fresh new air brought from deep in the Gulf. The salty wind spun and twisted my clothes about my body as I pleaded to Katrina. I hoped she was showing me the way. I was crushed, but free. I inhaled a cleansing breath. I would survive. I must survive. Genoa needed me.

The wind bombarded me with sand and debris. But I was still. I was motionless. I was in a centrifuge. Everything whirled around me, but I stood strong and alone on my slab inhaling the salty wet air deep into my lungs. I knew who I was. Even the winds of Katrina couldn't drag me into the muck and mud.

I bent to pick up the Waterford plate, marveled that it lay intact among all the wreckage surrounding it. It had been a wedding gift. I traced the inner circle with my index finger. I held the crystal plate close to my heart. Then I flung it as hard as I could. It flew far and deep into my pile of debris. I heard it shatter. I watched tiny crystal pieces break and dance among the ruins of my former life.

I screamed, "A house doesn't make a home!" into the remnants of Katrina as wet hair whipped my face.

Movement above caught my eye. I looked up. Jim was standing on his second floor back porch looking down at my slab. He didn't know I had made the trek down the road, and his eyes were filled with kindness. I waved a weak salute trying to communicate, "It's okay, and I'm okay." He and Laura already thought Conner was a bastard for not returning to help us, and I knew at that moment Jim abhorred Conner as I stood alone on my slab.

Jim came down the steps from his home. His front doors had been blown in and the bottom breakaway walls washed away as they were intended to do. From inside on his second and third floors, it didn't look like anything had happened. But once we looked out the window, trees hung with masses of unidentifiable cloth. And I could see straight to the Gulf, which had been obscured by a huge white brick home, just hours ago.

Jim hugged me so hard and held me.

I cried into his big, strong shoulder. Raising my wet face, I said, "I never liked that house anyway Jim. It was a 70s house. It needed more light." Motioning to my slab I pronounced, "Look, I've got a really great sunroom now."

He kept saying, "I'm so sorry," shaking his head. We walked back up the street with his big, strong arm around me, part comfort, part holding me up from the wind and the shock of it all. Rain soaked our clothes. My pants hung wet and heavy.

"We've been through a lot today, Jim. Hope you don't end up seeing my underwear too!"

We walked forcefully, heads tilted slightly down and against the wind and rain. His arm remained around me. We walked in step. We tried to take in all that we saw. Our heads turned together in time looking from one side of the Lane to the other. It was a gush of emotions, moments of awe, deep sorrow and loss, but also the tremendous relief that the unknown had revealed herself.

δδδδδ

The good and bad part about hurricanes is that you know about them well ahead of time. Maybe the same can be said about some divorces. It's not a tornado or earthquake that randomly strikes without warning. But it's also a long, torturous wait that may begin when the storm forms off the coast of Africa, travels west, into the Gulf of Mexico, and possibly turns north. It allows time to prepare, and to get out of harm's way. But now the wondering had ended. Bridal Lane would never be the same.

I kept thinking about my brick home and then my slab. I kept thinking about my marriage and then a divorce email. How one became the other would never be exactly clear.

δδδδδ

The next day, Jim, Laura, Genoa, and I returned to Bridal Lane early in the morning. We climbed over Melody's roof. Genoa and I returned to what remained of our home and neighborhood. I hoped to find something that would connect me to happy times in my former life. I wore Genoa in the Bjorn on my chest and walked with caution and sadness around the property. I was looking for pieces of my life I wanted to hold.

In the distance, I saw the Webers, both Jack and Mary, walking about the massive heap of their debris. The tears flowed easily from my eyes. They held their aged hands together, as they had for 60 years of marriage, and moved slowly about the place that was once their home. It was a perfectly sunny day, no humidity, with a wonderful breeze off the water as no houses remained to slow its path. If I closed my eyes it was the serene peninsula again. But instead I could not take my eyes from my neighbors, sharing their pain and aching for them as they slowly journeyed over the square footage of their foundation.

Decades ago they had retired to the coast. Their white stately home with bold pillars on the front porch greeted a circular covered drive. Atop was a turret reminiscent of a sea captain's home. In retirement, they opened a little music shop. It kept them young and active, traveling to shows to buy instruments, working with young musicians, hosting small acoustic performances on Friday evenings. The shop was only a few miles from their home and was their pride and joy. The shop, their white brick home, and the peace of the coast brought them happy productive years together as a loving couple.

Katrina tore their home apart, leaving a heap of bricks, furniture, iron works, paintings, dishes, clothing, and their lives strewn across their yard. Unlike many homes on the Mississippi coast whose concrete slabs had been wiped cleaned by a massive wall of water, their lifetime of memories and possessions collected during their world travels lay in ruin before their eyes in a huge pile of despair.

I was surprised my neighbor was wearing all white. Her white boots, which looked like winter snow boots, were topped with white fur. Her white pants were tucked into them, and a white pressed blouse was neatly tucked in her pants. The first few buttons of her blouse were undone, exposing her beautiful strong neck and upper chest, a product of her daily swimming routine. Her hair was fiery red as always. In the mostly grey and brown remnants of our neighborhood, she simply glowed.

Although I was secretly sharing and invading their painful moment, it was not their pain and suffering that drew me in – it was their love and affection. The way they touched each other, his hand on her back, her reaching carefully to show him something in the rubble. I knew love would carry them beyond Katrina's destruction.

I turned back to my tedious task and began surveying and cataloging what remained. A dress my mother and I purchased in Thailand wrapped around some pipes. There was a softball lying alone on the slab, a memory of my youth and all the coaching my dad had done. A little box lay in a crevice filled with marsh grass. I picked it up and opened it to find a little Indian anklet from my friend Pratima for Genoa. It was so tiny and had teeny little bells that still jingled sweetly when I removed it from the box. I handed it to a happy Genoa held tight to my chest. I found a picture of my godson Garet. He was the son of a college friend and softball teammate. My family and friends were there to help me through the wreckage. I was not alone.

Part 3

Clean Up

And then the dreams break into a million tiny pieces.
The dream dies. Which leaves you with a choice:
you can settle for reality, or you can go off,
like a fool,
and dream another dream.

NORA EPHRON

Heartburn

17
FAIRYTALE

Wednesday 31 August 2005

We had spent the last three nights with Jim and Laura in their little brick office, starting the night before the storm. But it was getting dangerous and scary. There was no water. I couldn't bathe Genoa, no electricity, sporadic cell phone service, diapers and food were quickly running out, with no sign of relief.

I piled Genoa, Sweetie, and the remaining diapers, water, and food into the car. We would drive five hours to Atlanta and get on a plane there to Connecticut. We originally had Labor Day weekend flights to Connecticut originating from Port City, which was now out of the question. The airport had been closed since before the storm and was now heavily damaged. We would catch the second Delta leg from Atlanta to Hartford. In the meantime, we would drive to Atlanta, stay with my cousins and spend the night in a home with running water.

The drive that day was eerie and lonely on the bright sunny highways. There were few, if any cars on my side of the interstate. Everyone had already evacuated north, was killed in the storm, or had decided they would stay and protect what was left of their possessions and homes in case of looters. On the southbound side, there was a parade of military vehicles every couple of hours. Probably relief supplies, but we know now not nearly enough to help all those in crises.

Luckily Genoa slept well in the car and Sweetie was happy traveling. It gave me some time to enjoy the road and time alone. Everyone I cared about knew we were safe, my sister had emailed everyone in my address book and it was a sunny, dry day with a wide open road before me. I didn't want to call anyone. Conner hadn't called me, and I didn't want to call him. He didn't deserve my time or energy. If he wanted to know about Bridal Lane, he could go see for himself.

I knew I was going somewhere safe, where my child and I could bathe, and I would soon be on a flight to see my family. The thought of being in their arms was too overwhelming to think about while driving. I could not wait to see them at the Hartford airport. Having a plan and destination comforted me, given that I suddenly was homeless and so unthinkably dependent.

I spent the drive listening to Jo Dee Messina and Annie Lennox. Jo Dee didn't settle; she didn't let men walk on her; she didn't have regrets, just memories and dreams. She wanted a man to stand beside her, not in front or behind her. Every song on her greatest hits album touched me that day especially 'Bring on the Rain,' *Tomorrow's another day/ And I'm thirsty anyway/ So bring on the rain.* I could still taste Katrina's rain and wasn't afraid anymore. 'I Wish' played over and over.

> *I wish you joy. I wish you strength. I hope you find*
> *just what you're looking for ... and I wish you still*
> *loved me.*

I planned to make a CD of the song over and over again for Conner. I felt forgiveness in this song, a closing, a peace. But tragically I already knew Conner would never find what he was looking for. It was a pitiful song speaking to me of all the talent and love, both mine and his, that he discarded so carelessly. He had been given such opportunities in his life and the gifts to make a difference. But he could not manage his addictions, and I could not manage him.

Annie Lennox's 'Bare' album was a master, with titles 'Bitter Pill,' 'The Hurting Time,' 'A Thousand Beautiful Things,' and 'Erased.' Just like Chris Botti, these women shared my pain and rejection. Annie sang to my core with every single song on 'Bare.'

Honestly, the things that you said/ go round in my head/ Still, it seems to be true/ that nothin' I do can influence you. Banging a hard beat with her on my steering wheel, I sang most of the drive. *You'll be sitting on someone else's couch,* I sang to the road and the sunny skies ahead of me. *Finally the truth has come/ Guess I knowed it all along.*

I was alone, in control, driving to my tomorrow. My whole life I'd been independent, physically and mentally strong, self-reliant. I always had plans, goals, and a method to reach them. I mapped a path and followed it, not perfectly but almost always successfully. Yet I was shaken by all that had happened in the past week and weakened reflecting on my life over the past year.

But, none of that mattered. I needed food, and would soon need more water for my baby. 'Simple pleasures' took on a different definition as humanity was stripped to its lowest common denominator; survival.

My cousins knew about the storm and the status of my home obviously, but I would have to tell them about Conner. My sister called with directions to Lisa and Tommy's house. They lived on the south side of Atlanta in the Fairytale House.

I arrived late in the afternoon, the sunset beautiful. I always loved that time of day. The change of light and the rose film that covered the earth were so comforting, and it seemed even lovelier than before all the destruction I had experienced. I turned off the highway onto a quiet country road with a gas station and convenience store. I made more turns, and the soft rolling hills of green farm land were serene and breathtaking. I hadn't seen green grass and homes intact in several days. I found their mailbox. The white house set back from the road. Green grass stretched in front, horses grazed, flowers bloomed, and a cross hung on the front porch. The image of their home in the sunset is still so vivid to me even though so much else is blurry. It was the most beautiful house I had ever seen.

Lisa and Tommy met me at the car. I'm sure I was a wreck with mud and muck up to my knees, my feet and toes still in the sandals I'd worn down to 22, my hair and face were a disaster, but I didn't realize it since I was so relieved and happy to hug them both. I didn't even hear a word they said. I saw their smiles, enjoyed their touch. I felt welcomed and loved.

Lisa and Tommy swept us into a perfect home, our few belongings carried inside for us. We talked with their children. The girls I hadn't seen in years were now teenagers, gorgeous young women, and their little son I'd last seen as an infant now five. It was a picture of the perfect family, a fairytale. Or was it like my life, a protected and guarded image only?

Genoa and I headed for the shower which was what I craved most; soap and water. I was concerned about Genoa's health. She was still in diapers and hadn't had a bath since Sunday. It was now Thursday. I'd kept her as clean as possible with wipes, but they can only do so much. Lisa gave me clean clothes to wear for bed.

In the shower, Genoa played with the soap and washcloth. I stood under the shower-head. My shoulders caved. The hot water ran down around my face, neck, and breasts. Eyes closed, I cried tears of relief and joy. I smiled and sobbed into the spray.

"We made it, Genoa," I whispered.

Dark water ran from my body against the cream-colored tub. I scrubbed the muck and mud from my ankles and feet. I found a line of mud around my waist. I scrubbed everything and then turned to Genoa. I held her naked body close to mine. I caressed and washed her back tenderly. I noticed my finger nails were dirty. She giggled and stuck her tongue out into the water. We played squishy bugs, squeezing water in our palms squirting it at each other.

I mashed the fresh towel into my face, smelling its cleanness. Feeling my clean hair, I rubbed my hands down my head and neck. I stared at my naked body in the mirror. I felt surprisingly sexy and beautiful. I was so happy. Was it because of my journey? We survived Katrina. This is what a Katrina survivor looks like? A bit too thin perhaps, but something intrigued me in my own eyes. They looked more interesting than before.

Genoa asked me to pick her up and look in the mirror. I wrapped us up tight together in my towel. We made silly faces, kissing each other. I kissed her everywhere. Every little inch of her baby skin smelled delicious. Joy. It was inside me.

We sat at the kitchen table with Lisa and her family. We talked about school and the horses with Tina and Alexa. I couldn't believe how much they had grown. When Conner and I met in Texas, Lisa, Tommy, and the girls were living there at the time. I spent almost every weekend swimming with these girls and getting to know them, but now they were young women. I wish I could have found more energy to give them. It was odd that my life had sort of come full circle since my last time with them.

After the kids went to bed, Lisa, Tommy, and I sat at the table. I had taken a shower, eaten some dinner and had a beer, but verbalizing the news for the first time in person to family I knew loved and cared for me was difficult.

"Thank you so much for this dinner and everything. You can't imagine what this means to me. And to be in a home and take a shower and eat warm food." I was shaking my head and smiling. "And your family, your girls are wonderful."

"You know if you ever need us, just let us know. It's so special to see you with my girls again," Lisa said.

"Amazing how much they've grown! Last time I saw them was in Texas the summer I met Conner."

"So, how is he doing?" Tommy asked gently, clearly curious why he was not with us. I shrugged my shoulders diverting my eyes down to the table where I fiddled with my beer bottle.

"You guys are gonna love this. Conner emailed a few days ago saying he wants a divorce. I don't really understand what's going on. I know he's living in Miami right now. He's been there for two months doing some trauma training. But we saw him, a couple, well less than two weeks ago for Genoa's birthday. My mom, the whole family, flew down for a little party and cake." I noticed my fidgeting and put my empty bottle down. "It's so out of the blue for me."

"Oh, my God, Julie. I am *so* sorry," Lisa said with a sigh, her head leaning to the side.

"So how long has he been away from home?" Tommy asked.

"He left the beginning of July. All the residents do this. They don't have enough gun-shots and stabbings at the hospital in Mississippi so they send them to New Orleans and Miami for a couple months. He was supposed to be back home the end of next month. I mean, things weren't perfect, but they never are, right?"

"What do you think it is? Another woman?" Lisa asked.

"I really don't think so, he's so awkward around women." But my mind started to consider it. "But who knows, really. It definitely doesn't sound like him on the phone." My voice trailed off as I continued, "No, it doesn't."

Tommy brought us all another beer.

"Julie, you know Lisa and I have had our problems. You know I've made mistakes."

Lisa was nodding firmly with her eyebrows raised. "It sounds to me like there's somebody else in Miami. And this is coming from a man who has been there."

"I don't know. It would be hard to imagine, because he's not ... he's not cool or something. He doesn't seem like he would cheat. I used to joke that I was more likely to cheat than he was. He's always been so honest, and he used to blush with a white lie."

I flashed back to Labor Day with him looking me right in the eyes. And the strange voice on the phone, I was not sure I knew him anymore.

"Julie, you have to think about yourself right now and that beautiful little girl," Lisa said, bringing me back to the conversation. "The reasons don't matter."

Tommy had both arms on the table and leaned forward, his hands folded.

"Trust me, Julie, when I tell you there *is* someone else." Tommy spoke slowly. I stared back at him, digesting his words, swallowing hard. He was so convinced. No other alternative in his mind.

"I know how men act in these types of situations," he concluded.

δδδδδ

I thought about our marriage vows, our virginity, our promises. Could it be possible? Could the man who at one time didn't want me to unzip his pants, be having sex with someone other than me? I thought about my recent visit in Miami less than a month ago. We had some good sex during that trip. Was it because we were celebrating our anniversary or had he picked up some new moves?

My decision to save intercourse for marriage was not a religious one, but one of commitment and faithfulness to a life partner. Conner's decision was more religious-based, likely stemming from his strict biblical upbringing. Maybe this choice had proven detrimental while he lived in the sexiest city in the world. I was still comfortable and happy with my choice to wait for intercourse. But in hindsight, I wished Conner had had more diverse sexual experiences before we met. Maybe that might have helped him skirt the 'grass is greener' phenomenon.

The control impressed upon Conner by religion during his childhood, followed by the control and rigidity of the military life, left little room for personal development and maturity. His life and career had been dictated, and he would merely need to follow the rules. Sadly, when the rules and training wheels came off, he didn't know how to balance. Maybe I misunderstood his goodness and tenderness. Perhaps he was afraid to do anything he wasn't explicitly told he could do? The good was an act, a masquerade because he was too afraid to explore. Tommy's naked honesty overwhelmed me. I don't know if anyone else could have said those words with more meaning.

"Tommy," I said nodding slowly. "You're probably right. We've lived apart nine of the last twelve months with his work. We've gone to visit him every other weekend, but I don't really know what he's been doing. I've been too wiped out with a newborn, no sleep. Hasn't really been on my radar to worry about that."

"Julie, you need to start protecting yourself, Genoa, and your future. This is time for defense. Have you hired an investigator yet?"

"No." I stuttered. "I wouldn't even know where to start."

"Do you know anyone in Miami?"

"My friend Jackie lives in Palm Beach. Maybe her husband knows somebody."

"And how about an attorney?"

Lisa and Tommy had weathered their share of marital difficulties and were very open with their wounds and healing. We tearfully talked, and they helped me think through my next steps, hiring a private investigator, a good attorney, and most importantly, protecting Genoa.

This would be the first of many conversations with friends that invoked dropped jaws, and tear-filled eyes as they looked at me in disbelief, and then to little one-year old Genoa.

"You mean he didn't come to help you?"

"He stayed in Miami Beach?"

"He didn't come to see the remains of your house?"

After the initial shock, people started asking the first two most obvious questions, "Is there someone else?" And "Did he even want to have kids?" Hard questions Conner would someday have to answer for Genoa down the road. I hoped she would be comforted or at least satisfied by his response.

Rejuvenated on the drive, refreshed with a shower and food, I turned to attack mode. I called Jackie in Florida to help me find a private investigator, my own PI. I made lists of all the things I would need to do to protect myself and Genoa, move money, collect bank and phone records, review insurance papers.

I barely slept, but fortunately Genoa did and Sweetie was mostly relaxed. I replayed the events of the past several days, weeks, and even months. What had my marriage become? Could Tommy be right about all of this? Was Conner really seeing someone else? Or multiple women? Or men? It was Miami Beach, the sexiest city in the world, and he had become someone I didn't recognize.

I spent the night at Lisa and Tommy's wondering what the hell Conner was doing, while I sat all night worrying about my short term and long term future. Why didn't he suggest Genoa and I come to Miami and live with him there for a few weeks while he finished out his training? Even if we were to be divorced, I was still his wife and Genoa would always be his child?

Tommy drove us to the airport the next day. I brought my bag up to the check-in desk. I quickly grew teary as I realized this was all Genoa and I owned. *I was carrying all that I owned.* It was an immediate and overwhelming feeling of loss.

I told the agent, "You simply cannot lose this bag!"

She glanced up from her keyboard as if to say, "Whatever lady, we won't."

So I turned on the not-so-Southern Miss Manners and barked, "I just lost everything in Katrina and all I own on the planet *is in this bag.* If Delta loses this bag, I will sue them for everything they have."

Immediately realizing how ridiculous, and pathetic this sounded, I swallowed my tears and begged with as much humility as I could gather, "Please, please, do not lose this bag."

I tried to hold back the tears. I could feel the gawks and hear the whispering nearby from thos who had heard me. She put a special handling label on the bag. Whether it was to appease me or not, I don't know, but I felt better.

Tommy worked for Delta and helped us through security, walked us to the gate, and held my dog in her carrier. He was incredibly thoughtful and sensitive to the entire situation. I couldn't help but think Conner had become far too narcissistic ever to be so accommodating. Genoa and I had travelled overseas twice and all over the US for conferences and my work in the past year. We knew our way around airports. Yet Tommy's assistance was so needed. I didn't want to say goodbye to him. Everything had become a struggle at this point, and having his compassionate companionship was invaluable.

I held Genoa and tried not to cry thinking about seeing my mom at the Hartford airport. I tried not to listen to all the people talking about Katrina. I wanted to cover my ears. I didn't need to hear people talk about the event - I lived it. I knew what it felt like to walk up a stairway to nowhere, to carry everything you own in a borrowed suitcase, and feel so scared and alone that the thought of hugging your mother brought you to tears.

δδδδδ

Thankfully, Genoa slept on the flight. I closed my eyes but didn't sleep. Sleep had become a rare commodity over the past week.

The flight landed on time. I could not wait to walk my heavy legs past security and to my mother. I had never craved her touch so much.

I lifted the backpack onto my back, heaved the dog carrier onto one shoulder, and put Genoa on my other hip. We made our way off the plane, and the tears could not be stopped. I kept trying to stop myself knowing I was a mess already. My nose started running. I had no way of wiping it. We came in at the last gate and had a long walk. I was exhausted and felt like I still waded through water. This was the final stretch in my journey home. Once with my mother I would be able to collapse and she would help me heal.

I rounded the corner to the main terminal, and Genoa was squirming to get down and stretch her legs. I knew she would want to hug Grandma right away too. My mom and sister Elizabeth waited for us as close as they could possibly stand. Mom's reddened face conveyed relief, joy, and pain all at the same time. Genoa reached to hug her, and Mom couldn't wait to get her hands on us both.

Now that I'm a mother I can better imagine her pain and her immense desire to take away the pain from me. It was so difficult to see her teary eyes filled with compassion, desperate to ease my hurt in any way possible. The last time I saw my mother was at the Miami airport after Genoa's first birthday. The last time I saw my mother I was happily married, Genoa had a seemingly caring father. I had a house and a job. Now, two weeks later I walked to her a changed woman, a woman who had experienced hurt and loss like never before. I was naked. Daughter walked to mother, with her own daughter. We three would heal each other.

As we hugged, I thought I would crumple into a heap. Genoa and I had made it home. Genoa and I survived the storm. We were alive. What our life would become didn't matter. For now, I was permitted to be weak. My family would take care of us.

We drove home from the airport, talking and chatting with Genoa. Mom had packed snacks, drinks and toys for us, and Genoa was happy. We talked about Lisa, Tommy, and the kids, their kindness and the warmth that I felt from all of them.

Mom told me all about the preparations she, Dad, and Elizabeth had made at the house for us. We would be living with them indefinitely, and they wanted us to feel as comfortable as possible. Friends, family, and colleagues from both Mom's high school and Elizabeth's engineering firm donated a crib, a stroller, sheets, clothes, and diapers for Genoa, toys for her, and clothes and shoes for me. It was incredible all that had happened in less than two days' time. People stopped all they were doing to help us and make sure Genoa and I had all we needed.

On the way home, Conner called. The service for our area code had been sporadic since the storm and we were only able to send text messages for a while. Anytime I had a window of airtime, I talked to my parents or sisters, making plans for my trip to Atlanta and then Connecticut. This was our first post-Katrina communication.

I really didn't have anything to say, so I said nothing but hello. One might think he would ask how I was doing or how his daughter was faring after all that had happened in the past three days. Or maybe he would have asked if Genoa had eaten, or how the dog was doing since she hated thunder storms, or any other dozen questions about our welfare.

Instead, his first question was, "Did you get the keys to the '61?" That was his most pressing question. Did I have the keys to his prized 1961 pink Cadillac?

I heavily and audibly exhaled and said, "Conner ... I can't talk about this right now. It's been an exhausting couple of days."

Then he started hammering questions, "What about the car? The house? What happened? What does it look like?"

My mom had to pull over since we were on our street and would lose phone service in about 10 meters.

I replied simply, "It's unbelievable."

I sensed puzzlement, almost disappointment in his voice that we were still alive. We had made it through Katrina. He sounded like he had lost a bet. He had been wrong. We didn't die in Katrina. We weren't washed away. Conner hated being wrong.

He started badgering me with questions about the divorce. He wanted to know about our insurance and how we would split things up. My mom and sister were looking at me in disbelief. I hadn't even made it to my parents' house yet, and Conner wanted to talk divorce and financial details. At the time I was still in such a daze, I didn't have much to say.

I should have said, "No I didn't get the damn keys to the '61, you selfish bastard. I was packing food for our daughter. And the fucking wall where the key rack hung isn't there either!"

When I think back, the bizarre conversation sitting in Mom's car was with a complete stranger.

18
A FATHER'S WISDOM

The next day, the florist called. They had a delivery.

"Will you be home later today?" they asked.

"Yes, certainly," I said. I had no energy or desire to be out and about.

When the doorbell rang, I received the lovely 'Petite European Basket.' Included was a note:

> *A new day will come, a new garden will grow ... Julie,*
> *you are the strongest woman I know, and an amazing*
> *mother. I am so relieved to know you are safe.*

Conner sent me a house plant? I don't have a house anymore! Was this a joke? Forget the house, I don't even have a window sill to put it on. What a ridiculous waste of money. A 'guilt gift' was what my attorney called it. Nobody else thought to give a house plant or anything the least bit decorative. Instead family, friends, and friends of friends flooded my parents' home with clothes, shoes, diapers, baby gear, strollers, highchairs, cribs, gift cards, cash, et cetera. Friends were even sending me notes from their bosses and chairs of their departments with employment opportunities, numbers to call, one-year-visiting professor positions.

And Genoa's father, a high school valedictorian, a distinguished officer, and a physician/soon-to-be surgeon entrusted with the care of human life, thought to spend five minutes online and order a house plant. The bill came to my email the next day since he charged the plant to our joint credit card. To me, this so-called gift was a true indication of how out of touch Conner was with reality and how much the alcohol was consuming his brain.

δδδδδ

I spent the next several days drafting a divorce document with Conner and my attorney, Robert, via email and phone. Robert was genuinely concerned.

He said, "Julie, most people don't go through one of these events in a lifetime and you've had both so close together. Is there anything I can do?"

He and has family lived in Jackson, Mississippi, which was in the center of the state. But Katrina's wrath had whipped apart homes and sent trees crashing onto homes hundreds of miles from the shore. He, too, was living among the destruction, and his compassion was so appreciated.

At the time, I joked that at least we didn't have to fight over who would take which couch. With nothing tangible to fight over, we would never have to meet to divvy up our stuff. The slate was wiped clean. All our finances and possessions could be communicated and represented on paper and via email.

Robert was available to me pretty much 24/7 during the next few weeks. We even worked together Sunday afternoons when he would work in the office after church and brunch with his family. I spent the next ten days on the phone from 7am until 7pm with my insurance company, the Red Cross, university colleagues, FEMA — the Federal Emergency Management Agency, my attorney, banks and investment companies, former neighbors, mortgage companies, and trying desperately to reach coastal friends I hadn't heard from yet.

My sister Elizabeth took some time away from work. She became my personal assistant. She dropped her life for mine. She had all my identification information and was making file folders to help me stay organized. Christine had begun a highly competitive, condensed nursing program. She wanted to come home and help, but we all told her she needed to be in school and be productive. This program had been her dream, and I certainly didn't want her to sacrifice any learning time. Mom, Dad, Elizabeth, and I, along with all our friends, were tackling the immediate needs and divorce issues.

We needed to move quickly so Conner would no longer have access to our joint credit cards, a large home equity loan, mutual fund accounts, and Genoa's savings account. At that point, we did not know what he was capable of and only knew I needed to protect whatever Genoa and I had left. Elizabeth was most efficient and made lists a few times a day with calls or notes I needed to make and send. She and my mother organized the donations and gifts people brought by the house, her office, or Mom's school. It was a full time operation with dozens of boxes, deliveries, bank checks, cash, and dinners coming to the house every day for the next few weeks. It was truly an 'It's a Wonderful Life' moment. All the people whom my mother had helped in her life through her volunteer work, high school friends of mine, childhood friends of my sisters', co-workers at Elizabeth's engineering firm, university friends of mine, other teachers at Mom's high school, friends of friends, and bosses of friends at large companies like MTV and BCBG – it was overwhelming and impossible even to keep up with who sent and brought what to the house.

δδδδδ

Our friend Marian stopped by to bring a meal for the family and some items for Genoa and me. Marian was a longtime family friend. She too was married to a physician, an oncologist who worked long hours. He was forever giving to others in a difficult field where cancer all too often won the battle. Marian was trained as a nurse and highly intelligent. She had organized and run an outreach program for underserved communities that could not get access to immunizations and healthcare. I knew she would be the one to ask for help.

I had not yet mentioned anything about Conner to anyone but my family. The outpouring from the storm, the loving emails, notes, and gifts, were already too much to respond to at this point. But people kept asking, kind of concerned and also oddly curious, "Where is Conner?" Or in one email a friend wrote, "Conner must be worried sick about you. I can't believe he's stuck in Miami Beach all alone." And another, "I can't believe the military would keep him there in this type of crisis." It was getting to the point where people would have to be told what was going on.

The "poor Conner" bit nauseated and infuriated me. And I was beginning to doubt Conner was "all alone" in Miami Beach. The late night unanswered phone calls, "I'm too tired to talk tonight," and the continual cash withdrawals and credit cards charges were all highly suspicious. I now had some distance and time to reflect upon all the pieces. Wedding band left behind, boob job and sex-every-day requests, the divorce email, the conversation with my mother. Not returning to help us evacuate, "Where are the insurance papers?" coupled with "I'm so worried you're going to die!" abandoning us after the home was destroyed, and the final "You should stay in Connecticut, that's the best idea." Probably much more was going on than I would ever know.

Immediately, mine and Genoa's health were critical. We had visited Conner ten days ago in Miami Beach. I had sex several times with him during that visit. Who knows what he'd been doing in the 'sexiest city in the world?' I needed to get tested for everything possible.

Marian walked out the front door down the brick walk as my mother and I were saying goodbye.

I hadn't discussed this with my mom and blurted out, "Marian, I need to get some tests done. Do you know where I can go for AIDS testing?"

She looked confused, and her expression said, *Why would Julie need an AIDS test?*

I added flatly, "Conner's probably cheating on me."

In her typical, get-it-done-fashion, Marian gave me the name, number, and address of a testing center where the results would be anonymous, and I could make an appointment to be tested in the next few days. She would call ahead and explain the situation.

As if thinking about all that I had lost, calling the Red Cross and FEMA for any assistance, arguing over finances with Conner, securing an attorney, moving and protecting money for Genoa, considering other employment options, and calling the mortgage company weren't all enough for me, now I would have to submit to and await blood test results for a slew of STDs.

All I could think of was Genoa. I washed her in the tub every day. She ate food off my fingertips. What if I had a paper cut? I changed her diapers, and sometimes she had little abrasions or rashes, had she been exposed to anything? Might I have given her something? I had to blot out the thought; it was too much to handle. If and when the news came I would deal with it then. I had always been skilled at compartmentalizing my life's issues and prioritizing. This was now on the closet shelf and would be addressed later when more data came in.

δδδδδ

I hired a private investigator in Miami Beach to follow Conner on his nights off. My attorney suggested we get any information about him possible, since it was beginning to become clear he had been leading a completely different life in Miami and hiding things from me for months.

The PI was a retired cop from New York City, named Mike. His thick Brooklyn accent was layered with decades of smoking. He sounded like a well-worn, experienced man, who had seen much of the underbelly of humanity. I explained my situation and told him our goal. I wired him money, faxed him photos of Conner, the make of his car, his phone number, et cetera.

It was exhilarating compared to the lengthy hold times on the phone with FEMA. We were in close touch for a little over a week, which was plenty of time.

I called him as soon as I knew Conner was off work or would note he wasn't online anymore and would probably be going out to dinner or a club.

Mike would always close out conversations with a deep and raspy, "Okay, love ya, baby."

I quite enjoyed associating with him and the whole secret world of investigation. My whole family started saying a raspy, "Love ya, baby," after everything. It was some comic relief we all desperately needed.

I also began printing out phone records from Conner's cell phone and calling all our credit card companies to get current statements faxed to the house. Who was he calling, what times, what was he buying, when, and where? I was in protect-and-defend mode.

Elizabeth and I began long hard searches online given that Conner had casually suggested that I go online and check on Yahoo! Personals and single ads a few days ago. What was *he* doing online? There it was, in late June, a charge on his AmEx for FriendFinders.com and another charge the following day to Yahoo Personals. In June? I guess he had some time to kill. He was obviously thinking about divorce, or at least adultery, long before his email August 24 and well before we celebrated our seventh wedding anniversary together on July 25.

After hours of searching and many laughs in the process, we found Mr. 'MiamiBeachFunTime.' His introduction was, "I want to be 100 feet tall in love." The only criteria for his date: "Age 18-33, Body Type: Voluptuous." I could instantly tell by the wording that this was Conner's ad without a doubt. It was sad. A typical ad might read something like, "I'm an avid runner, play piano, and love my work as a software engineer. Thought I would try this online dating thing to test the waters. I enjoy cooking and eating Thai food and am looking for a dinner companion." Conner's ad read:

I am a courteous but not wimpy man that rarely yells, gets upset and yells, but am passionate about many things. I would love to find a sensual woman for multiple dates and maybe more if our chemistry is right.

Tragically he described himself as "Separated" with "No children." We tracked his activity on the site, and it turned out he logged on every day, even in the days immediately after Katrina when he claimed to be too busy to be able to help us. He had also joined other singles sites that were more explicit and sexual in content. Whether it is online pornography, sex in the media, or sex in sitcoms, the general ubiquity of sex in society seems to cultivate the notion that "Everyone else is having better and more sex than I am." For an insecure man like Conner, this somehow reflects poorly on their masculinity, as if sex and only sex defines their existence.

Mike and his partners staked out his condominium and were able to follow his car down to the strip on several evenings. They followed him into clubs and bars. In the days immediately after Katrina Conner charged dinners over $100 on our joint credit card, spent most of the evenings out, and was 'sleeping' in places other than his military, government supplied condominium. An officer at best, a gentleman no longer.

But the phone calls with Mike kept me smiling, and I was always warmed by the not so velvety, "Talk to you in a couple hours. Love ya, baby." And we did talk at all hours of the day and night. I was beginning to learn about all that Conner was doing when we weren't physically together. It would be years until I would learn much more about what was going on while I innocently thought he had to, "Get back to the patients."

δδδδδ

The Red Cross sent a volunteer to my parents' home to meet me. When Marnie appeared at the door, I had difficulty placing her. Then I realized she was the mother of a girl I played basketball with in high school. She was compassionate and helped me get several hundred dollars in assistance immediately. I was surprised to hear how many Katrina victims had evacuated to Connecticut. And even though the circumstances were unpleasant, it was a nice surprise to reconnect with someone from my distant past to remind me once again I was not alone.

The Federal Emergency Management Association - FEMA to those of us having to rely on them for services – became a household name after Katrina. Due to their non-action in New Orleans, the term sadly became synonymous with how unprepared the federal government was to deal with a disaster of this magnitude. Dealing with FEMA was a bureaucratic nightmare. I registered with them online; I registered with them twice over the phone, and still they didn't know who I was when I called. I answered their survey questions dozens of times over the next several months, with ridiculous questions like, "Did you evacuate?"

I wanted to yell, "If the house was destroyed and I'm alive, I must have evacuated. This is not a rigorous proof, people!"

Answering this question several months after the storm was laughable. Then there were a slew of house description questions. "How many TVs did you own?" "How many phones?" "How many radios?" This was how they determined the value of your contents. It seemed an extremely shallow quantification of the actual value of my possessions that didn't include estimates of things like my shelves of books, computers, cappuccino machine, Wusthof knives, my Grandfather's violin, skis, et cetera.

I received my first FEMA letter in October informing me I was 'ineligible' for any assistance because I had 'Insufficient Damage.' I was shocked. Insufficient damage? What would be sufficient? Did I have to be dead to be eligible for assistance? I continued to get these letters every six to eight weeks.

Several months later, in the spring I met a FEMA employee on my now empty lot at 22, and I answered all the same survey questions again. This time I watched him enter them on his tablet PC, but still no change in the outcome. In the next year and a half I continued to receive letters informing me that I had 'Insufficient damage.' I received 14 of these letters. It was disturbing to read that FEMA was investigating a possible $485 million that was misappropriated as a result of Katrina when I completely lost my home, was a single mother who had to live with friends to maintain my job, and received nothing. However, I was not surprised given the complete incompetence I experienced.

I heard FEMA was hiring employees at $40/hour to work tables and help victims complete paperwork. Businesses in town were having a difficult time keeping their office employees because of the high FEMA pay. My colleagues at the university asked, "Do they have a need for a Ph.D. in history/French literature/geography?"

Thankfully, Governor Barbour, the Mississippi senators, representatives, and mayors were working around the clock. Many of them had also suffered losses. Senator Trent Lott grew up on the coast, and he too suffered a total loss to his home and property. Fortunately and in stark contrast with what was going on at the national level and in neighboring Louisiana, Mississippi's state relief efforts were organized and more efficient.

δδδδδ

The days and nights that followed at my parents' house were a haze of horrific conversations with Conner about the divorce, Genoa, and our finances. I sat in my father's home office with Conner on speaker phone, taking notes, and allowing my family to hear him. His complete lack of conscience and ability to totally relinquish any responsibility for his wife and child was unparalleled.

He even asked during one discussion almost wistfully, "Julie, what is love?" Surely he was inebriated.

I replied, "I might have had this conversation years ago, but I think we're past that now, don't you?"

He then became an utter freak show and I had to cut him off. It became harder and harder to believe I married and loved a man like that.

From this point forward, I understood arguing with him or pointing out his multiple downfalls would gain nothing for me and for Genoa. Now was the time to cater to Conner as best I could and feed his narcissistic ego without giving ground on a comfortable future for Genoa. Now that divorce was in my future, I wanted it to move as quickly and efficiently as possible and be done with these erratic and tragic phone conversations. If that meant coddling him for a few more days and weeks, I could do that.

Mississippi does not have a 'No-Fault' divorce. One of us would either have to claim fault or we would file jointly. I struggled with this. I didn't want a divorce, but Conner would not be able to find fault, such as adultery. But filing a joint complaint to dissolve our marriage was breaking my promise, "til *death* do us part." Yet filing jointly would be the most efficient and painless way for us to move forward into our new lives.

Our biggest commodity, as is the case for most people, was the home we 'owned' on Bridal Lane. We didn't really 'own' much of the home at all since we only were able to put 5% down and had a 30 year mortgage we'd only been paying for four years. Now that there was no home, property values were unpredictable, and any insurance payout would be months, possibly years, down the road, if ever. Deciding what to do with this unknown commodity was difficult. I knew the potential insurance payout could be significant, but we also had a large mortgage and high interest home equity loan for the addition. Selling the property and splitting the gain would take longer than I wanted this divorce to take. I needed these agonizing drunken phone calls to end.

After much discussion with my attorney and my family, I told Conner that 22 will have to be a package deal – the mortgages go with the insurance money. So one of us will have 22, end of story. The paperwork involved would take much longer than either one of us wanted this marriage to last. And I was not going to spend hours and days on the phone with insurance adjusters, forensic engineers and architects, possibly go to court against an insurance company and then give Conner half. I predicted he would probably claim to be 'too busy' with work as usual and the logistics and insurance battle would fall completely on my shoulders.

I wanted 22, but knew it would be a risk. And it is still a risk for me to this day. Insurance costs are high, if any are securable; taxes are increasing, and building costs are almost prohibitive.

I'm a mathematics professor, a quantitative, logical human being for the most part. But 22 is the place where I read on my swing under the live oak watching pelicans soar, did some of my best academic work, earned my first big national grant, looked up from my coffee each morning to see dolphins swimming in the bayou, enjoyed a glass of wine on the pier at sunset, and later brought my newborn home to her first bedroom.

Genoa experienced a breeze for the first time with Grandma on the swing hanging from the tree in that yard. Even though the house was gone, I had so many memories of my gorgeous surroundings that were the beauty of that home. The flounder, redfish, shrimp, and crabs were delicious, and the serenity of being able to look far across the water to the other shore relaxed my eyes during long days of research. I wanted the peace back that I found at 22, without Conner, without the drinking, without the bad memories, and despite the risk.

We spent the next week on the phone and email drafting and redrafting a divorce agreement. We made decisions and agreements on everything from savings accounts to how to pay for Genoa's future orthodontic work if needed. The document was detailed and would guide our future interactions and Conner's visitation with his daughter. The days and nights were exhausting. My family read through each draft and everyone had feedback and suggestions. It was amazingly comforting to have all these loving hearts and brains focused on the future for Genoa and for me.

I sat in my father's home office late one night after I had completed everything on the day's list: provided new documentation to the insurance company, faxed and emailed slab pictures to FEMA, checked in with neighbors about their progress, requested more back phone records, called to talk with my department chair about plans for the semester. Conner and I were finally done nitpicking about the divorce details.

I sat in Dad's swivel desk chair. My fingers ran up through my hair, above my ears and sat crossed atop my head. I leaned back and looked around the little room. Dad's degrees and awards hung on the walls. As did a framed quote I'd given him for his birthday a decade ago.

A Message for My Father
How can I find the words to let you know how much
I care? To thank you, Dad, for all you've done, for
always being there … You've been "friend" as well as
"father" walking with me all through life, through the
joy and through the laughter and through the heartache
and strife. You're the best I could have hoped for, and
with gratitude I see … the sweet lifetime of devotion you
invested here in me. I am proud to be your daughter,
thankful for the times we have had, and with all that
is within me I feel blessed that you're my dad.
I love you!

Upon his desk were gifts from his three daughters. A pencil holder carved in middle school wood shop, a painted rock, a framed photo of the three of us from Father's Day, a picture I took of him during his trip to Florida with my college softball team, a painted paper maché container, a mouse pad graced with Genoa's face – all the treasures of a beloved Dad and Grandfather.

My dad was not a perfect man. But he had been an exceptional father, a strong and honest role model for his three daughters. And he was a faithful husband to my mom. They stayed true to their vows. Their wedding prayer, which was part of my wedding ceremony, hung at their bedroom door.

In my vows, I promised to be with Conner in sickness and health. Conner was an alcoholic; a functioning alcoholic, one who was performing surgery on soldiers every day. But without a doubt Conner was an alcoholic. He had a disease. Was I doing the right thing by agreeing to divorce him? Was I breaking my vows? I sat in Dad's office, a place of stability, central to our home, off the kitchen, and read the 'Message for My Father' again and again. This was the first moment since August 29 I entertained anything but divorce.

I left the office and slowly walked up to the family room.

I stood on the stairs and asked my family sitting around the couches, "Do you think I'm doing the right thing by divorcing Conner?"

They all looked at me like I was crazy. I continued, "Well, he's obviously ill. This is a disease he has. In my vows, I promised 'in sickness and in health.'"

After all the grueling and abusive conversations they too had endured over the past weeks, they were surprised by my inquiry. Frankly, so was I. In many of the conversations, it was clear he had been drinking heavily and he sounded so frighteningly similar to his father when he drank, like a drunk, angry teenager without the ability to reason or carry on a coherent and connected dialogue. But somehow I still felt sorry for him, his disease and his clumsiness, knowing it was all a horrific waste of talent.

After a few moments of silence, Dad said, "Julie, you don't have a choice here. Conner doesn't want help. He wants out."

Dad was so clear and direct, like Tommy had been. And I knew it was true. I wanted out at that point too. But I wanted to know if philosophically my actions were just.

Was this the right thing to do? Would Plato and Aristotle have declared my actions ethical? Would Genoa in the future agree with my decision? Did my family think I was doing the right thing? We had never discussed all of this. We let Conner do the driving that began with his divorce email. True this did not seem like my decision to make, but was I right to go along? I had agreed with so many other things I didn't want to do in this marriage. My alignment with and signing of the divorce documents would indicate my approval or at least agreement in ending our union and ultimately breaking my vows.

I wanted to be like my parents. I wanted my vows to be important and meaningful. Even though I knew Conner had already broken his marriage vows to me, two wrongs do not negate each other. I needed a better resolution to have peace in my mind and harmony with my choice.

I went back down to Dad's office. Back in his swivel chair, I looked back on the artifacts of the life and family he had grown. Love was displayed in this room. I cried into my hands leaning my elbows on his desk. Tears flowed and I smeared them into my unkempt hair and wiped my nose into my shirt sleeve. I stared blankly into the glow of the computer screen and thought about other friends who were divorced.

My friend Jackie shared a wonderful poem with me by a Cuban poet her first husband had given to her years ago when we met in New York. I lost my copy in the storm. He described love as an entity we create and groom outside of ourselves. It is a relationship and being that exists philosophically and essentially physically in between two beings. It requires continual cultivation and nourishment. When one party is no longer nourishing the being, it dies. Therefore, love is not about the person who is doing the loving, or the person they love and adore, rather it is about the entity, the space, and time you give to that relationship that grows between two people. If one lover moves or steps away from that entity it no longer exists in its original form. A one-sided marriage or love affair could not last.

And so was my case. I'd been left alone to choose between nourishing a dying entity and nourishing my young child. I would not be able to do both. Genoa needed me more as a mother than Conner needed me as a spouse. Sitting in my dad's chair surrounded by his history, I felt a finality and sense of comfort about my decision. I had my rationale and it was one I could defend.

19
RUMMAGING

I'd been anxious to get back down to Mississippi and see if anything could be retrieved. But we didn't want to begin the clean-up and have Conner change his mind and decide he wanted 22. Once it was established the property was mine, Dad and I drove down to Mississippi and began the process of salvaging. Genoa would of course come with us because I couldn't be away from her for days.

My family had all seen pictures of the property now, but I knew seeing the devastation in person would be incredibly exhausting for us both. But Dad was always willing to do anything for his daughters. He had been a father to three girls, the best a daughter could possibly hope for. He had been supportive and sensitive, courageous and consistent. He wanted to help in any way possible and a trip to Mississippi would provide a physical task to do in a situation where I'm sure he felt otherwise mostly helpless.

Dad and I went to Home Depot in Connecticut to buy a wagon so we would be able to haul things as needed. We also packed the car full of tools: shovels, sledge hammers, picks, and rakes. We weren't sure what we would need to sift and dig through the remains. We packed lots of water and juice and enough work clothes to last us about a week.

I had spoken to Genoa's baby sitter in town, a high school senior named Amy. She and her mother had offered to watch Genoa during the days so Dad and I could work on the property without worrying about all the dangers of nails, pipes, gas lines, and glass present on a ravaged property. I was extremely grateful they were available and willing. Without them, the process would have taken much longer or I would have had to leave Genoa in Connecticut. She was much too young to be away from me for so long. I took attachment parenting seriously - I was her home. As a result she was such a secure little person, confident with a wonderful sense of herself. I didn't want to risk any emotional strife that could be prevented. This would allow us to work on the property during the mornings before the sun got too brutal and spend the afternoon and evenings with Genoa.

It was a long drive from Connecticut to Mississippi with a one year old. Luckily she was still a good car sleeper. I read her books from the front seat. We all sang songs. When Genoa slept, I amused myself sketching possible house designs, and Dad and I talked over various ideas. We later measured the lot dimensions and took breaks imagining where a new kitchen might be. Our trip was an emotional father-daughter journey. Dad and I both were wary, but looking forward to doing something physical and making a tangible difference.

We packed extra fresh fruit with the hope that Genoa wouldn't get constipated with all the sitting in the car. Unfortunately, the exact opposite happened. She loved grapes and ate red grapes much of the drive. I hadn't thought anything about it until she began crying while she pooped. She screamed in pain, like never before. Her diaper filled with red grape skins. She ate plenty of green grapes before but for whatever reason her body was not breaking down the red skins. The poor little thing cried in pain every time she pooped for the next day. Dad and I felt horrible. She was in so much pain passing those skins. Dad would start pulling over when she cried so we could comfort her as much as possible. She eventually would pass them all, but it was a difficult drive for us all.

We spent one night in a hotel and got down to Mississippi the next day. We began seeing damage hours before we reached the coast. Trees had been devastated and signs battered in the winds. The breadth of the storm was absolutely incredible. I talked with Dad before and during the drive about the destruction, but nothing could prepare one for these sights. It was impossible to comprehend the damage until you had driven the miles of despair, viewed the acre upon acre of debris, and walked among tattered children's belongings, shattered families' dishes, and photos smeared with mud.

We pulled off the highway. Dad's word choice was no more eloquent than mine was on the 29th.

"Oh my God, oh my God," he said.

Even weeks later, it was as if the storm had just hit, except some roads had been cleared leaving debris piled high to the sides. We drove down Bridal Lane first. By that time we could drive all the way down the one lane street.

I wanted Dad to feel comfortable being emotional and let him grieve as I had done. He too had happy memories of the home and the family of three that used to live there. He got out of the car first, and I let him walk a bit on his own. Genoa was fortunately asleep in the back seat. Dad walked up the steps and stood on the slab, his feet spread. One hand cupped his elbow the other hand covered his mouth. I could see his face redden as we all do when we cry. He held his nose. His mouth dropped as he continued to gaze upon all that was once my home. I hadn't seen my father cry often. A sentimental man, he teared up at sappy movies, but rarely expressed pain or sadness with tears. He did at that moment. I followed slowly behind, placed my hands on his back, my head down between his shoulder blades. He turned and grabbed me by the shoulder. We hugged and held each other.

"Julie," he sobbed. "We'll get through this. I'm here now, and we'll get through this together. We're all in this together. And now this place is yours. We'll get you through this." He softly repeated the mantra. "We'll get through this …"

It was painful sharing this setting with a family member for the first time. Just like it was difficult sharing news of the divorce for the first time. Now it was public and again there I stood naked. At least now there would be someone else who could talk about 22 and what they had seen. Dad had relieved more of my pressure within.

We spent the night at Karen's family farm house, north of I-10. Dad, Genoa, and I moved in on her and her dogs. It was hotter than hot, no air conditioning, and the large bugs seemed to have moved in long before we did. The ceiling fans provided some relief humming above overhead.

Karen, a biology professor, and I had been in touch right after the storm. She lived a few blocks off the beach. Her house had been spared except for some flooding, but her neighborhood was now closed to the public. The neighborhood was blocks and blocks of sweet little beach houses with front porches, hanging plants, bikes leaning on the sides of homes ready to cruise the beach. Now the homes were barricaded by the National Guard. Entrance required a photo ID and barbed wire surrounded the entire community. Bodies were still being found. Some houses had only been flooded, and a structure still stood while other clusters of homes were piled in a debris heap, in some cases stories high.

The National Guard presence, the uniforms and weapons, the barbed wire made the ghost town feel third world and dangerous. We gained access to the protected area with my university ID so we could assess the damage of my office and campus. I hadn't had time to clean out my belongings there, but had hoped that, with a second floor office, things might be salvageable. We reached the highway that ran parallel to the beach and drove in silence viewing the miles and miles of desolation and destruction. Semi-truck trailer frames bent around trees, cars upended in the sand, live oaks' sprawling branches covered with debris, barren house slab after slab to our left and beautiful beach stretched to lapping waves and pelicans to our right.

I saw the university signage in the distance. My office was on the second story of a building at the south side of campus, closest to the beach. I could sit at my desk looking through the live oaks to the beach and Gulf in the distance - hard to imagine a better office setting. We turned onto the campus and my building sat before us. The first floor washed away and pieces of the second floor flooring hung exposed. But I looked up and had hope. The three arched windows of my office looked intact. I wished we could enter and see what of my former life remained in my office, but it was getting late, and we needed to get back to Karen's.

The next morning we went to the grocery store to buy food for Genoa and brought her to Amy's house. They too had damage. They lived on my bayou just further east, their house set higher. But they were living in disarray as their first floor had completely flooded. The overall structure was not damaged, but floors and drywall would need to be replaced. They lived a new normal as well and yet still offered to help. I was so grateful to them. Genoa would be in loving hands while we worked, safe from the harsh remaining elements of a shattered Bridal Lane.

The task ahead was daunting. Now that we were there, now that the place was mine, where should we begin? For me, the most tiring part of working at the slab was that my eyes were continually darting from one item to the next. It was hard to focus. The combination of stress, exhaustion, heat, and sorrow made my head spin. Working in one area I could see an item a few feet away and move to that area to see if anything was salvageable. It was difficult to follow individual tasks through to completion.

We wore gloves to reach under broken glass and lift bricks. We began sifting. We used the sledgehammer to break up remaining pieces of the exterior walls that had fallen to the four sides of the slab. It appeared that the second story new addition had been blown off into the marsh, where all the master suite contents and hardware laid, and then the four exterior walls fell outward.

The carpeting had been pulled from the foundation and was tangled about the bricks that were my fireplace and mantel piece. We were able to wedge a crowbar under the fireplace and rescue some of my grandmother's dishes. I loved these dishes. They were the English castles. My mother told me that her mother never liked them and called them her 'ugly pink dishes.' But to me they were 'red on cream' and matched perfectly with my red, black, brown, and gold living and dining rooms. I was so happy and surprised to have found some intact. An antique soup tureen sat completely unharmed as did a bottle of Jack Daniels as if knowing we might need a swig or two while we rummaged.

Jim and Laura gave us a key to their house and let us use the ground floor for sun coverage. Dad and I took breaks, hydrated, changed clothes, and showered one afternoon at their house. It was amazingly unharmed, looking like a new beautiful showcase home. I knew Jim and Laura felt sad and guilty they had been spared, compared to many friends and neighbors. Katrina's damage and the aftermath were cruel for so many different reasons, but everyone suffered. They owned a flooring business and were needed immediately by the community. Many people whose homes remained needed new carpeting, new tiles, new rugs and Jim and Laura helped them get their homes and lives back to normal.

A few days into our arduous task, we decided we would need something to clean the few items we had found. Jim and Laura loaned us a wheelbarrow they had salvaged. We bought some bleach and some toilet brushes and filled the wheelbarrow with water and bleach. We attempted to disinfect and semi-clean any items we decided were worth saving. Laura hailed this the 'White Trash Dishwasher.' We washed my grandmother's china in a wheelbarrow. Oh my, what would she say? Laura came over and took our picture.

A sporadic stream of gawkers drove by while we worked at 22. My neighbor, Melody, dubbed them the 'Lookie Lous.' People would slow drive down Bridal Lane looking at all the destruction and despair. It became entertainment for some, with most taking photographs or shooting video from their car windows. Bridal Lane was a tight community and even more so after the storm, so it was easy to identify the Lookie Lous.

The worst case happened one Sunday afternoon when a car parked at the dead end of the street. Two women and at least 5 children piled out of the car laughing and talking. They all had cameras or video cameras in their hands. I tried not to look at them invading my neighbors' grief and taking pictures of their exposed lives, their nakedness. They hadn't hurt anyone, I told myself. I put my head back down and continued working in my rubble with hopes of finding bits and pieces of memories or special items to hold onto.

I found some broken toys of Genoa's and a few pieces of one of her puzzles. She loved her puzzles. I squatted beside my slab, and looked up to see these little children coming up the street, closer now to my property, playing, running, and taking photographs. I stood up holding Genoa's three puzzle pieces, my arms at my sides. I wiped the dirt and sweat from my forehead with my forearm and fixed a long stare on one of the mothers. I rubbed the puzzle pieces in between my fingers. I waited to make eye contact. I wanted to look at her, mother to mother. I wanted her to understand. I waited.

"That's it," I said under my breath.

"What, what did you find?" Dad's voice hopeful I'd located a precious artifact.

"Nothing, Dad. I'll be right back," I said with my head jerking in the direction of the Lookie Lous.

"Why, where you going?" he said as he stood.

But I didn't answer. I was already walking deliberately and largely in their direction. I had been thinking about what I would say to these people, these invaders.

I approached one of the mothers after I watched her take several more pictures while I walked toward her. I was dirty, scruffy, with scratches all over my arms and legs, face sweaty and smeared with Katrina sludge. I looked worked over, but I felt strong. I would protect my nest.

I reached one of the mothers, stood between her and the property she was photographing and said calmly and sternly, "I would like you to leave this place." Pause. "I would like you to leave my street. Right now."

She looked shocked. And then she appeared confused and almost inquisitive.

I spoke slowly and deliberately as if making a speech to large crowd of Lookie Lous.

"This is not fun for us. This is not entertainment. This is my life. And I do not appreciate *you* being here invading my grief."

Both women were entirely apologetic, bowing and ashamedly shaking their heads. They left more quickly than they arrived, piling their quieted children back into the car. I walked back toward the slab. I walked a bit taller than before. Dad watched me return to my piece of earth.

A neighbor, rummaging through his ruins, lifted his wide sunhat and nodded as if to say, "Thanks. Well done, girl."

Soon after this episode Dad, Melody, and I fashioned a sign from a piece of wood debris. We placed it at the entrance to Bridal Lane blocking the left lane of traffic. It read,

"Bridal Lane Residents Only.
Violators will be prosecuted, by order of the Police."

We had a great time exerting our non-power, laughing and cackling while we created the notice. The sign lasted for a few weeks and kept the Lookies away for a while.

The next day I had my first meeting with an insurance adjuster. A young man, about 22, drove up with another young man who looked barely 17. They both appeared genuinely sad and concerned.

"I'm so sorry about all this, ma'am. Did you have flood insurance?"

I looked defensive I'm sure, raised my eyebrows and told him, "I would like to discuss my wind policy."

"Certainly, why don't you walk me around the property."

The adjusters had obviously been well coached on how to react and interact with policy holders. We walked over the property a bit, and I explained to him some of the remains and showed him evidence of wind damage.

After about 15 minutes of him being very polite and acting sympathetic, he said, "Ma'am this is going to be a long slow process. Right now you can go downtown to the local office and get a check for $2,000."

I looked at him wide-eyed and said, "$2,000? My annual policy, that I just paid, costs me over double that. Until you have a six figure check I don't want anything. What is two grand gonna get me?" I asked, gesturing to my slab.

As kind as he could be, he told me that was all he could do. He would talk to his superiors and explain my situation. I was not only homeless, but had also become a single mother with a one year old daughter, and I was paying a large mortgage for a house that no longer existed. I needed help.

And yet so many people were in worse situations. I had family elsewhere and a place to go. In some cases, families lost three or four homes and had nowhere to turn. My friend Lucy and her husband lost their home as did her parents who lived down the street. Another friend lost several homes on a family compound together. Many Mississippi families lived within blocks or miles of each other. If one house got hit, in all likelihood so did their brother's. It was the nature of living in a place with roots.

Dad and I finished up the recovery at 22 faster than we had thought. Sadly, there wasn't much worth keeping. After a few days of scraping, unearthing, and lifting we had collected only two recycle bins full of items. They were mostly silver serving pieces, a few pieces of pottery, and a handful of my grandmother's hated dishes. We were also able to salvage some of the iron patio and deck furniture. The chairs were scarred and bruised, but so was I and they could still provide a place to rest, like the stump in 'The Giving Tree.'

Towards the end of our workdays, Dad and I set these chairs on the slab and enjoyed the sunset. Despite the wreckage and trampled lawn, there was still a beautiful image of what was and what might be again. We sat and rested our tired bodies and minds. Such an exhausting task, with so little reward, we collected just two bins of so-called keepsakes. We bought and set up a new mailbox at 22, now that mail service had finally resumed. I hoped it was the beginning of something more.

One afternoon, as I rested on the cleared slab, I could see above and beyond the debris strewn across my yard to the peaceful marsh grass and a small pond shared with my neighbor.

In a breathtaking moment, I caught a glimpse of a female snowy egret. The beauty and elegance of the white feathers stood in striking contrast to the blue-grey brackish water of the bayou and multitude of greens found in the marsh grass. My eyes scanned the marshy pond and soon after, I saw her partner coasting on the breeze. He landed beside her. The wedding white brilliance reminded me of Mrs. Weber's boots and love's sweet purity propelling humanity through despair.

I looked to the horizon, breathed in the lightly salted air, and remembered what drew me to this place and why I still felt so connected to the sea. I knew in that tearfully joyous moment, life and love would return to that place in many forms and so would I.

20
A NEW NORMAL

Conner called in late September, his voice unusually gentle and kind. He called to ask a favor. His medical training program would be closing on the coast. Conner needed to find another place to finish his training. He wanted desperately to stay in Miami Beach.

Desperately he said, "If they move me to Ohio I'm going to die there. I need to stay here."

He begged me to call his superior officer to encourage his stay in Miami. I'm not sure why he thought I would have some power over this decision-making process. But he told me that Colonel Johnson had the impression that we might be able to salvage our marriage if Conner moved out of Miami. I didn't think Miami Beach was a good place for him to remain. It didn't seem good for his mental or physical health, and I told him so, but I agreed to call Colonel Johnson.

Colonel Johnson and I discussed our marriage briefly, and I let him know it was irreparable. We both thought it would be best to have Conner on a military base where his actions and behaviors could be more closely monitored. Within a week Conner was moved out of Miami Beach.

My university decided to reopen in October two months after Katrina ravaged and destroyed much of the campus. It was an incredible timeline and people were working around the clock to get ready for our students to return.

I had been living in Connecticut since our salvage trip to 22 and our stay with Karen. Classes were to begin again, but we had no place to live. The university had been working closely with FEMA to provide temporary housing to all the faculty and staff left homeless but the trailers were not yet ready. We heard that they had the trailers but had lost all the keys.

Dr. Manuel Moser, a psychology professor, and his wife Angela called to offer a spare bedroom in their house to Genoa and me. They offered their other bedroom to another university colleague. The Mosers were a young couple that had moved to the states from Austria a year before and had recently purchased a new home. I would also need daycare since I had lost my nanny and would be living in another town. Angela offered to watch Genoa while I was teaching. It would be as good as possible given the circumstances.

On the phone while I was in Connecticut, Manuel had only one concern. "I don't think it will be possible for you to bring your dog. We have two cats."

His generosity and tenderness almost brought me to tears.

"Oh my, Manuel, Sweetie can stay here in Connecticut with my parents. You are so kind to even think of her!" They not only considered my needs and my daughter's needs, but also my dog's needs.

They were incredibly sensitive and welcoming when we arrived mid-October, the day before classes began. Angela had made a delicious dinner the night we arrived. They were vegetarians, so we ate fabulously healthy meals during our stay and Genoa always had fruits and vegetables available to her.

Classes soon began. Repairs and construction were ongoing. A library and computer facilities were established, rooms and spaces were carpeted and painted, furniture was salvaged and delivered, white boards were installed, small laboratory facilities were created, et cetera. It transformed before our eyes. Construction continued long after students returned. We lectured and tested with the sounds of drills and hammers in the background. But everyone understood. If we wanted education and learning to continue we needed to make some sacrifices. And we all did. This would be our new 'campus' indefinitely.

The Bush and Clinton Relief Fund provided tuition for many university and college students affected by the storm. Students might have lost their home, vehicles, jobs, and even loved ones, but they could continue their education and pursue new careers. I saw Presidents Bush and Clinton speak together the following spring at Tulane's graduation ceremony. The work and fundraising they did for the coast was met with extended applause, banners, and multiple standing ovations. They had been here on the ground frequently, working together across political lines. They helped Americans who had been battered by nature and supported New Orleans, an historical treasure left in crisis. The energy they exuded that day was like none I had ever experienced. I was in the presence of tremendous leadership. The power rippled through the audience. And the former presidents' humorous barbs and jokes were hilarious for the two former competitors. They were inspiring.

I spent my days teaching and then picked up Genoa. We tried to spend as much time out of the house as possible. I didn't want to exhaust our welcome in any way and I thought bringing a toddler into a home without children might be overwhelming. Debris still littered the beach and most of the parks, making outdoor play dangerous. We, along with the rest of the coast's population, spent lots of time at the Wal-Mart since it was the only place open. The whole notion of killing time and waiting for life to switch back to normal was torturous at times. I looked around, and people were zombies. But I thought about how wonderfully equalizing Katrina had been. There was no white trash or black trash or yellow trash. We were all just zombies in Wal-Mart.

I stood there one time staring over the lobster tank holding Genoa. Is anyone even buying lobsters right now? Another mother, obese, with gold and missing teeth, and two children in worn clothes, crowded loudly around the lobster tank with us. Our little girls shared giggles. We shared a smile and a moment that only mothers can, enjoying their children enjoying childhood.

We had all been through so much together. So many people were now in some sort of cramped living arrangement, whether with friends, in a trailer, or in a hotel room. Although depressing, I felt more comfortable being back around other Katrina survivors. We spoke the same language and had a shared history. We knew not to ask questions like, "So how are your repairs coming along?" or "Are you back in your house yet?" Nobody attempted to comfort with, "Well, you had insurance, right?"

A sense of community had blown in with Katrina. People were broken and their sad eyes dark with exhaustion, but we smiled with understanding when we passed one another. A connection and kindness had taken root.

Despite the high gas prices, we hopped in the car for takeout, grocery shopping, mail runs, whatever. My car was the only space I could actually call my own. In addition to our Wal-Mart journeys, Genoa and I made regular trips back to Bridal Lane. I carried her around the property and collected our mail. It not only gave me a destination and time killer, but kept me connected to the place I loved.

One visit I pulled in front of my mailbox and saw a new addition to my slab. Gray-blue, it looked like a statue perhaps. I reached my arm into the mailbox eyeing the figure in the distance. I wondered who left it and what it was. I didn't recognize it. I walked closer. A figure of a standing mother in a long dress holding a small child stood before me. It was not mine, but someone must have thought it was. I thought of the sculpture of the family of three that once sat on Conner's dresser. This figure was the shape of my new life. Tears rolled.

I picked her up with both hands. She was heavy. The mother stood 12 inches tall. The width of her dress at the bottom was four inches in diameter. She was large and sturdy. Her cheek leaned onto the child's head. She comforted the child with her whole body. Arms wrapped one around the baby's bottom, the other her shoulders. The mother's shoulders rounded, her whole torso cradled the child. The child's face was against her mother's neck and chest, both arms up by her eyes, like she had been scared. Every detail was familiar. I ran my fingers over them, cleaning out the Katrina muck.

Who put this here? Where did she come from? Neighbors would leave items for each other if they recognized them, or thought they did. Genoa was the only baby on the Lane. Maybe someone guessed this was mine. She was made of red clay that I could see toward the bottom. The blue paint looked to be worn off exposing the burnt orange-red around the bottom half of her skirt, making it look that she had been splashed by mud. Calm tears dripped for this metaphor, awe over this beautiful gift standing on my slab. I put her carefully on the front seat, next to me, and took her with me.

δδδδδ

Conversations in the hallways on campus were no longer about the next conference we were attending or 'brilliant' publication we had in press. Instead, faculty members exchanged numbers for forensic architects, the governor's assistance hotline, and the local church's hot free meal schedule. We shared survival stories pre and post Katrina. Nothing was private.

I chuckled repeatedly, "Nothing is sacred anymore when your underwear is hanging in your trees."

And that was the case for so many of us. Surviving the storm for most, was the easy part. The grueling challenge came in the form of living and plodding along every day after the storm. We all worked to keep each other up, celebrating small successes together like the day someone got $700 from FEMA. Such were our victories. But a strange utopia of sorts began to congeal.

Formal professional relationships became friendships greeted with hugs. Everyone hugged and held hands. We all needed affection and the healing of human touch. I often brought Genoa to campus. Her little giggles and immunity to post-Katrina depression uplifted us all. She became a mascot of sorts after the storm, coming to most, if not all, of the campus and department meetings. Most of the time she sat entertained with her grapes, blueberries, and a bag of books. My colleagues became accustomed to her attendance and periodic interruptions of, "My turn to talk," or a random, "Why that man have a beard?" in a not-so-subtle toddler way.

The second weekend of classes, Mark and Olivia, whom we had traveled to New York City with, offered their home to us in Hattiesburg. They were away for the weekend, and we had the house to ourselves. They had no damage, and since their daughter Sophie and Genoa were the same age, there were toys and books galore for Genoa to enjoy, a changing table, bath toys, and swings outside. It was one of the best gifts I have ever received. I know at the time they didn't realize what a comfort that was for us. A weekend of quiet time alone for us was an amazing two days of rest and rejuvenation. In addition to their home, we were also able to shop in the nearby stores that had reopened. What a luxury to have a place other than Wal-Mart.

We flew back to Connecticut the last weekend in October and thanked Manuel and Angela for their incredible and timely generosity. My parents had finally closed on the house they were supposed to close on right before Katrina. The house received no damage, but the home the current owners were building had, hence the delay. But Genoa and I were going to have a home to live in as of November 1!

The purchase of this home had been fortuitous. Dad had visited the previous summer to watch Genoa while I conducted some mathematics workshops. In the late afternoons, we would sometimes drive around and assess area real estate to see if anything struck a chord. They had not planned to purchase a home at the time, but when Dad and I pulled up to a beautiful Mediterranean style home, we called the number on the sign to get the price. A woman answered. She was both the realtor and owner offering to show us the home right then. The price was reasonable, the house immaculate. I took some photographs for Mom. Soon after, they bid on the home. Now Genoa and I would live there.

Dad, Genoa, and I made another long journey from Connecticut to Mississippi, this time *sans* the red grapes! We also took Sweetie. She slept most of the trip in Genoa's wagon. We gathered camp chairs, a television, inflatable mattresses and bedding. The rest of it would fall into place. I had no furniture, but that didn't matter. Genoa could run around, we would have a yard, and I could bring my dog back to the coast. It was a relief.

I bought a mattress off the back of a truck around the corner from my house and a couch and loveseat from a guy who pulled up in a semi from North Carolina. Trucks like this periodically appeared with all kinds of furniture and rugs. I purchased a set of chairs and table for the kitchen from Target with gift cards from friends, and bought a few kitchen items. That was all two people really needed.

I brought the mysterious statue into my new home and placed her on the kitchen counter. She was dirty and needed washing. I placed her carefully in the sink to give her a sponge bath. I didn't know what the statue was made of and didn't want to damage it further. The Katrina mud rinsed onto my hands, down the drain of the white sink. She was bluer than she appeared at 22. In the folds of her dress at the bottom, I could now see the artist's name, Lily Grace. The 80 year old woman who had lived across the street made this with her hands. She had a beautiful studio in her home and worked in multiple media – oils, watercolors, marble, and more. But I'd not seen any sculpture like this before. A noted Mississippi artist, this must have been an early piece of hers, made by young novice hands. I called her daughter, also named Lily, excited to tell about her mother's piece found on my slab. These small victories were reason to celebrate.

After I told her about the figure she said, "Julie, we are moving Lily to an assisted living up north now."

"Is she doing okay?"

"Actually she's doing quite well. We just thought this would be a good fit for her. Give her some social life and get her away from the coast for a bit."

"Oh, good to know. I know this has been terribly difficult for your Mom. I remember her stories of Camille."

"You know, Julie, I think she wouldn't mind one bit if you kept that figurine. I'll check with her, but she would probably be happy you and that sweet baby are enjoying it."

"Really? Goodness, Lily, I would absolutely love to have it, but, well, how about I just hold onto it for you? You know where it is when you want it. I'll take good care of her."

"I know you will. Now you take care now, okay?"

"Thanks so much, you too. Hugs to your mother."

I dried her off and smiled, still amazed that this piece found its way into my life. I had an empty fireplace mantle. Mother and daughter would be the first to grace that space.

21
DISSOLVED

A Judgment of Divorce in Mississippi takes sixty days once filed with the courthouse. They give you sixty days so you can think it over, I guess. I suppose it took me longer than that to plan my wedding, so it only made sense the legal system wanted to save time and trouble by requiring you think it over at the other end.

On a warm, sunny morning in December, Genoa and I arrived at the makeshift courthouse temporarily placed in trailers on the fairgrounds. Dozens of trailers held city and county files and offices. I had some difficulty finding the correct trailer but was in contact with my attorney by cell phone on our way. He drove three hours down from Jackson, Mississippi.

Genoa and I entered the trailer and her cute smile, big blue eyes, and blonde hair always demanded attention. She said hello and then quietly sat in the front row of folding chairs where I set her up with some books while Robert and I stood in front of a table where a judge sat.

The judge asked, "Is your marriage reconcilable?"

I said, "Excuse me?" not understanding this question. After he repeated it, I shook my head slowly with a definitive, "No, sir."

I couldn't wait to have this marriage officially dissolved. And that word 'dissolution' was so appropriate. It described what had happened to my husband – he had slowly dissolved into something I no longer loved or even recognized. Conner didn't appear at the proceedings.

My attorney and I talked as we walked out to our cars.

"Why did he ask if my marriage was reconcilable?" I inquired.

"They are required to do that here," he explained.

I guess it was to make sure I was of sane mind and capable of verbal response. I was certainly sane, possibly more sane and lucid than I had been in years. It was one of the fastest divorces my attorney had ever seen.

My former neighbor chuckled in his deep southern drawl, "Julie, if I ever need a divorce, I'll know who to call!" He had been and remains happily married to his wife of 35 years.

Nevertheless, I cried leaving that makeshift courthouse. It was final. I was driving home a single mother. "Is that all it takes to change the life and future for a child?" Genoa rode happily in her car seat looking at one of her books, not noticing my tears.

She would be okay. *I* would be okay. And *we* would be okay.

The man I married dissolved. Now it was time to focus on the best of my former marriage, Genoa. The words from the song by Andre Deluca in the past tense rang true, "Yes, in Genoa love *was* alive."

δδδδδ

I saw Conner shortly after the divorce for the first time. He came to Connecticut to pick Genoa up mid-December. He would be flying to Chicago with her to his brother's graduation ceremony. It seemed more of the charade and upkeep of appearances. He wanted to appear the good father at the family event. This was especially the case since his twin had a baby girl as well, and Genoa's great-grandmother would be there from Los Angeles. Conner hadn't seen Genoa for more than 12 hours since August and Hurricane Katrina. What would he possibly do with a one year old child he barely knew at a law school graduation ceremony?

He got out of his rental car in the grocery store parking lot, looking like Mr. NASCAR himself. A tight black leather jacket with Budweiser embroidered across the back, slicked hair, tight jeans, and cowboy boots. I hardly recognized him. NASCAR, really? I found this garish red and black costume, paired with his exaggerated movement, reminiscent of the Phantom prancing in the masquerade scene of the Phantom of the Opera.

Just like the Phantom, Conner lived in layers and layers of masks. All the new clothes, while Genoa and I still suffered and struggled. He was a caricature of the man I married. His expressions, clothing, and swagger all unattractively exaggerated. Maybe he was trying on another mask, to see which one fit this situation, always the chameleon, never comfortable in his skin. I was extremely concerned about leaving Genoa with him, but I knew he had legal rights to see his daughter. I was somewhat comforted there would be other adults around at the graduation and tried to remember that he was a physician and imagine that he would be able to care for at least her basic needs.

After she was loaded into the car seat, he asked, "Do you want to have dinner when we come back?"

Surprised, I asked sarcastically, "What would we talk about, the menu?"

Taken aback by his question and even more surprised when he asked *again* when he dropped Genoa off. I didn't understand his motive whatsoever.

I asked him flat out, "Are you trying to get back together with me?"

"I just thought it would be good for us to talk about some things."

"We've had plenty of time to talk over the phone in the past few months. I don't really have anything to say to you … Besides, we," I looked at Genoa, "Want to spend time with family."

Once again, I was unaware of his plan.

21
A NEW YEAR

I decided to throw a party and had invitations printed, reading, *We could all use a little extra holiday cheer this year!* It was a wonderful event and people dressed to the nines. With so many people still homeless and fighting insurance companies, even by December few people were back to pre-Katrina normal. We all talked of the 'new normal.' Everything had changed, and life would never ever be the same on the coast. My parents came down from Connecticut to celebrate.

We lived in a lovely home. Mediterranean in style, with an open floor plan, high vaulted ceilings; it was a beautiful place for entertaining. Many of my friends, former neighbors, and university colleagues were still living in trailers, hotels, or with family or friends even now, months after the storm. Being homeless was an odd feeling - without a space to be, to sit or to rest. It reduced human beings to a raw common denominator and in many ways leveled the playing field. As a way to say thank you to all my dear friends and ring in the New Year, or more accurately ring out the old Katrina year, I threw a holiday cocktail party on December 30. New Year's Eve always seemed a dangerous night, so we decided a New Year's Eve Eve party would be best.

That evening we shared the beautiful home we were so fortunate to have and drank to the New Year and our new lives. A New Year that we hoped would be without hurricanes. Some men wore suits, some women evening gowns. People were so happy to have a formal event to attend. It was fun to get dressed up since clothing post-Katrina had become so insignificant. Neighbors and colleagues who formerly never dressed in anything but a skirt or suit, now wore jeans and sneakers to work or shorts and T-shirts to the store. Even if they had received nice clothes from friends or relatives or had the money to replace their wardrobes, dressing nicely was almost an insult to those who had lost everything.

But the night of the New Year's Eve Eve party, people dressed to impress and celebrated the end of 2005 and all the great plans we had made for our new lives and our new normals.

My colleague laughed, "I can't believe everyone is ironed!"

Connection and ties we felt for each other were like no other. All our homes had been shattered to nothing. Our belongings scattered in our yards and into the Gulf. We had all been reduced to our naked selves. No one could hide behind their possessions, beautiful landscaping, home furnishings, and real estate. Katrina served as a tremendous normalizing event. We were all now just human beings each trying to figure out next steps, sharing tactics and plans. Competition had disappeared. There was no keeping up with the Jones.

While we all suffered in different ways, we all had a shared memory, a shared language, and a shared vision of hope for our future. As the population shifted with more casinos and condominiums, the typology and landscape of the region continued to change. I will always feel a connection like no other to the friends, neighbors, and colleagues who suffered as well. It was an entire community of survivors. They too knew what it was like to climb stairs to nowhere.

I felt like I was living in utopia. Significant remnants of that goodness and kindness from neighbors, friends, and strangers in similar predicaments remained and hopefully always would. The Coast indeed would never be the same.

23
THE ANNIVERSARY

One year had passed since Katrina ravaged our shore. It was a truly difficult day. One of the casinos, The Beau Rivage decided to boldly reopen on August 29, 2006. It was something we all sort of looked forward to, regardless of people's views about gambling and its booming economy on the Coast. The local media covered the anniversary for almost a month leading up to it. The national media covered the anniversary, but it seemed by then, many people in other areas of the country were tired of hearing about it.

I wrote a letter again to attempt to thank and touch base with all my friends and family.

> *Greetings,*
>
> *What a year it has been! The Katrina anniversary was a difficult time here on the Mississippi Coast. So much has been lost, changed forever, and countless tasks remain undone. Many places still look as if the storm was yesterday. For me, the storm's anniversary was a period of reflection about the incredible power of the ocean, the quick and unexpected changing tides of life, and the overwhelming goodness human beings can bestow on friends and strangers alike. Genoa and I have innumerable things to be thankful for, among*

them your friendship and assistance that carried us through the storm's aftermath.

I spent the day on August 29th retracing our steps of a year ago, allowing myself to remember and re-experience all that I witnessed, smelled, and felt. I visited the little brick house where we evacuated with our neighbors and spent the eerie days after the storm. I drove down my street, stood on the property on Bridal Lane remembering walking up my front steps to nowhere, and enjoyed the cool breeze on the now cleared lot, thankful we made it through the last 12 months. There is nothing physically there yet but the plans are coming together. Fortunately Genoa, now two, is too young to remember what once stood there, but old enough to understand we're going to "house, build it here by mailbox soon!" Other neighbors are also rebuilding. Some will even be back in their new homes by the holidays. It has been inspiring to be a part of the rebirth process and witness friends' and neighbors' tenacity and focused desire to return to the place they call home.

I am writing to thank you for getting me through a very dark and difficult time in my life. When I think back to my parents' Connecticut living room filled with baby clothes, toys, books, towels, sheets, clothes and shoes for me, gift cards for every store on the planet I'm simply speechless. Friends of friends of friends sent clothes to Genoa and gift cards to us. We couldn't even keep up with the postal service! Your kindness and compassion cannot be described, and I will be forever grateful. It was and remains entirely overwhelming. You not only helped us, but I was in turn able to share so many items, money, and gift cards with other Mississippi children and families in need. Your generosity is still echoing as we pass clothes and toys Genoa has outgrown to those still struggling, and your donations are helping to rebuild a bridge.

We plan to be part of an exciting future here on the coast. It will not be recognizable in five years time. The university plans to rebuild the beachfront campus and also expand to an additional location to accommodate the amazing influx of people following the casinos, condominiums, and construction boom.

My employment is secure, and the opportunity to be part of the redesign of a university and its campus is a unique and exciting circumstance. We have now also received some insurance money, and I am currently working on house plans. I hope to break ground next summer. The lot has been cleared, and the driveway and concrete slab demolished. We are finally ready for a very fresh start! I guesstimate we'll be back on Bridal Lane mid 2008.

In the meantime, we have a very nice place to live temporarily. Genoa is taking music classes, learning to swim, loves going to the beach, and cannot do enough puzzles each day. Thank you for helping in a multitude of ways, get us back on our feet and whole again. Among the many things Katrina taught me, is that life is about relationships and nurturing the people and relationships you love. Thank you for loving us!

With love and endless thanks,
Julie and Genoa

δδδδδ

I was filled with hope even though the surroundings were in some ways more depressing than they had been in a year. As the anniversary passed, friends and colleagues were in some cases more depressed that there had been so little progress in 12 months. Where is my insurance money? Where is my contractor? How am I going to send the kids to college now? A whole year had gone by.

Ads on the television and radio offered free counseling and help, warning that the anniversary might bring some of the most difficult times for people in our area. And truly it was. Several friends went on antidepressants. Many were still taking sleeping pills and liquor stores seemed to be the most lucrative business on the coast.

I was so thankful to have Genoa in my life. She kept me going. I couldn't crawl into a hole. I couldn't drink until dawn. I couldn't go out to bars and casinos. She woke me up at 7 am every day, her happy little self wanting to read books.

One morning I almost cried. She walked up to my bed, put her little soft hand on my cheek while my eyes were closed, and said, "I love you too, Mommy." That is without a doubt the best way to wake up. Her books and her smile were priceless in those slow dark times.

People might think life would have been easier if I'd been by myself, without another person to worry about. But in truth having someone else to care for took my mind away from the tedious phone calls and destroyed contents lists required by insurance adjusters. She also reminded me to take time to sit on the floor and play with blocks, Play Doh, puzzles, and roll in the grass on a daily basis. These would not have made my to-do list if I didn't have a toddler. She kept my heart and soul alive.

My house design for 22 continued to come together. Fortunately, since we were still in the house my parents bought, and they were not kicking us out, I was in no rush to start building. I took my time designing something that was perfect for 22. I walked the property daily and envisioned rooms in different locations, decks, lanais, windows here and there. Having a challenging project energized me.

I decided to start small by doing the pier first. My father and I designed this. I wanted a fisherman's perspective and knew once again he would have some great ideas. It would be a great place where we could enjoy 22 until a house was built. We designed a large roof to cover two boat lifts. I didn't own a boat yet, but we were planning for future possibilities. There would be ceiling fans, lighting, a sink, cutting board, and a built in bench. Although a relatively small project, it took months to complete. But it still today provides a beautiful place to enjoy the egrets, mullets, and sunsets again with my sweet Genoa.

24
KEYS

As I close this chapter of my life, I have experienced, seen, felt, and learned an incredible amount in such a short time. In some moments, I've lived and experienced much more than a lifetime. In others, I am brand new – at life's beginning. I know I certainly never imagined this would be my life's path. Sometimes I shake my head wondering, "How did I end up here? This was not in the script."

Most importantly I have learned a great deal about humanity, its capacity for goodness and its underbelly. Tragedy, destruction, and desperation inflicted by Katrina brought people to the edge of compassion. There they decided whether to pursue goodness or retreat. It might not have been a conscious decision, but nevertheless decisions made in times of crisis reveal one's true character and core. I witnessed people hoarding, people suffering, people giving, people loving.

When nature takes all infrastructure away, the human mind realizes and becomes more aware of its basic mammalian needs, as if left in the wild without preparation. Most Americans have never experienced the fear and desperation that surfaced. A fear that the world would never return, that life will never again be 'American normal,' that we were helpless victims of nature.

Horrific evil also snuck in because the world had essentially stopped turning. No one was watching, no one would be held accountable, and no one would know what had happened. People trolled Bridal Lane stealing treasured belongings. I cannot fathom stealing crystal and silver from elderly people who lost their homes. You know who you are.

This was what most of the world witnessed on CNN in Katrina's aftermath. It's almost impossible to believe that human beings could behave in that manner. But unless you were here in the heart of the destruction, where the storm raped and ravaged the planet, you cannot understand the breadth of emotions and mental anguish the human animals left behind experienced.

δδδδδ

The most critical thing I learned is to be as self-sufficient as possible. Especially as a woman, I have and never will rely on or expect someone else to support me and my child financially. I never imagined myself divorced. No one in my family had ever been divorced. Even if they silently considered it, they were Catholic. Divorce was *not* an option. Nor did I ever dream I would be a single mother. If a child were involved, divorce *could never* be an option.

In my case, divorce was not my choice, nor was it an option. Conner emailed me clearly. He didn't want to be married to me anymore, and he didn't want help with his addictions. The method was unusual, yes, but the outcome was familiar to many.

I was fortunate. I had a job, one where I could be at home with my daughter, bring her to meetings when needed, work full-time with flexible hours, and also be a full-time mother. When Katrina took away my earthly possessions, I lost my diploma, but I still had my education, my mind, and my knowledge. Education is the only thing you can ever truly call your own. No *one* and no *thing* can ever take that away from you.

δδδδδ

People ask if I'll ever get married again after such a shocking and sudden end to a nine year relationship. Fortunately, I've had two good relationships since the storm.

One was with a man named Steve from New Orleans. He proved that a man could still be a wonderful companion and, even more wonderfully, that someone else is capable of loving Genoa almost as much as I do.

My second relationship was with a surgeon. He taught me two seemingly divergent lessons.

The first was that I will never date another surgeon. Their lifestyle and the professional community in which they function do not seem to cultivate honesty and fidelity in personal relationships. The divorce rates are high for surgeons. I don't think that the field draws people who are naturally primed for failed relationships, but instead the intensity, stress, and surroundings create an environment where commitment and faithfulness to one's partner are more difficult to maintain.

The second lesson was that I am still capable of falling completely in love and letting myself be loved. This was amazing to me. After all my heart and mind had suffered, I was able to trust again. Love does indeed conquer it. I have enjoyed loving and sharing parts of my life with someone else. I love feeling loved.

However, that said, as a single woman I know I can always count on me, period.

Overall, I have fewer disappointments. Someday I would like to share an honest, productive, and supportive relationship with someone. But for now, raising my daughter, helping students, and growing into more of myself sustains me.

I married a masked man. Conner did not know who he was and still struggles with his troubled childhood and the skeletons he stashed. The children of alcoholics have difficulty maturing past the age when the effects of alcohol entered their lives. They also desperately seek the approval of others. Conner probably desires to be a good human being, but is sadly a master chameleon with codependent leanings. He changes to accommodate any particular situation, hiding even from himself.

I will have difficult questions to answer in the future from Genoa. But I have been honest with myself, my family and friends, and most critically, I have protected and supported my daughter. I have operated sincerely and with integrity and am grateful I had the strength and role models to help me make the right decisions and choices. I do not believe in heaven or hell. But I do believe in justice and balance. Time will bring us balance, it always does.

Both Katrina and my ex-husband altered my life in dramatic ways. But in both cases, I was made better. I didn't want to be married to an alcoholic, nor did I want to raise Genoa around the behaviors that are associated with that disease. I also don't ever want to surround myself with 'stuff.' It too, can dissolve into the wind or the ocean. Instead, I actively choose to fill my life with fulfilling and enlightening activities and travel, and surround myself with other people also trying to reach their dreams.

On a recent return flight from Connecticut, we sat next to a man who asked Genoa, "So what do you want to be when you grow up?" She was not even three and had yet to be asked this question so I listened, intently curious about her response.

"I'm going to be a woman!" she said.

"Good idea," he replied smiling. "And what are you going to do?"

"I'm going to help people!" she said.

I beamed with pride. How could I hope for more? I want to help Genoa fulfill this dream and others like it that will hopefully make the planet better. She will make a difference! And I hope the utopia we experienced post-Katrina can be the 'new normal' for more people.

δδδδδ

It is June 1, 2007, the beginning of hurricane season. I cleaned out a purse yesterday that I had evacuated with almost two years ago. It was filled with cards from friends, miscellaneous snips of paper with phone numbers of neighbors, colleagues, insurance adjusters. It had been hanging on the door of my closet for over a year. I obviously hadn't needed or wanted anything in that purse. But today I finally decided to clean it out.

Reading through the old notes from friends was uplifting and brought me quickly back to that week in August 2005 that now seems a lifetime away. I unzipped a little inside pocket, found two keys on a ring by themselves. I rubbed them in between my thumb and forefinger. I tried them in my front door, but I already knew they wouldn't fit. These were keys from my former life. I sighed and smiled. They had no use anymore. They would never open another door for me. It was a bittersweet reminder of all that was lost, and yet all that had been cleansed and reborn.

I wasn't ready to part with them yet. These keys once opened the front door to my baby girl's new and perfect life. I put them into the back of a drawer. Maybe I will find a lock to fit them again another day.

EPILOGUE

My husband and I went sailing today with our two daughters Genoa, nine and Lill, two. He's a scientist, giver, reader, learner, thinker, coach, a strong father, and my true partner. He gets me. He loves me. I adore him. I treasure him. He's confident and sexy. He's comfortable in his skin. He is honest, consistent, and imperfect. He's the one I want to have coffee with on Sunday morning and every morning.

We became a family at 22 Bridal Lane in December of 2009 after meeting on eHarmony in the Fall 2007. It was a chilly sunny December noon. Few remnants of my slab remained. The pier and boat house stood in the distance. We hung a new swing from the live oak. The bayou was high, the winds light, and the marsh grasses golden browns. Our friends and family stood circled around us.

The first few months we dated I thought, *He's so normal. This is so easy.* I thought that would end. It hasn't.

My wedding band is 32 tiny diamonds around my finger. I asked the jeweler in town to put his best stones in it.

"We usually don't use that high of quality, since the stones are so small. You really won't know the difference," he said.

"Thanks so much," I said. "But *I* will."

Conner was married again. He was divorced again.

My mother died. Breast cancer crept its way into her lungs and spine in March 2008. She died August 1st that year. I am now a motherless daughter. I grieve.

My father is my rock. He continues to live in Connecticut and still loves fishing on our pier when he visits.

My daughters, Genoa and Lill, are beautiful and brilliant. They are terrific little women. Women, I hope, who will grow up and help people.

A new garden has grown.

If you enjoyed *Naked*, please consider leaving a review. Thank you!